2-6-63

262

DATE D

MAY 8 '70

D1541496

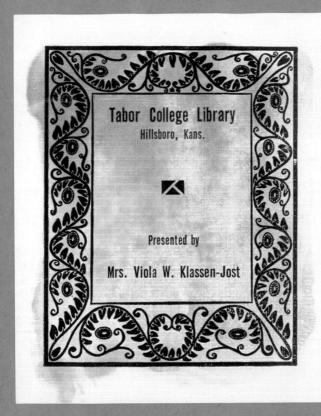

Tabor College Library
Hillsboro, Kans.

Presented by

Mrs. Viola W. Klassen-Jost

DO YOU KNOW?

- WHY FAMILY BANKRUPTCIES ARE HIGHER TODAY THAN IN THE DEPRESSION
  (See Chapter I—*Enter the Debt Merchants*)

- WHAT PSYCHOLOGISTS SAY ABOUT CREDIT CARD SYMBOLISM
  (See Chapter II—*The Rub in Aladdin's Lamp*)

- WHAT PRIVATE CREDIT AGENCY HAS MORE INFORMATION THAN THE F.B.I.
  (See Chapter III—*Big Brother's Big Brother*)

- HOW COLLECTION AGENCIES USE PSYCHOLOGISTS
  (See Chapter IV—*The Specialists in Friendly Anxiety*)

- WHY WOMEN ARE BETTER THAN MEN AT FINDING DELINQUENT DEBTORS
  (See Chapter V—*Finders, Keepers*)

- HOW OUR SCHOOLS HELP SPREAD CREDIT IGNORANCE
  (See Chapter VI—*The Wonderland of Credit*)

- WHERE 12 YEAR OLDS ARE ALLOWED TO BUY ON TIME
  (See Chapter VII—*The Pied Pipers of Debt*)

- HOW TO BUY "INSTANT" MONEY
  (See Chapter VIII—*From Kimonos to Instant Money*)

- HOW BAIT ADS PULL IN CREDIT CUSTOMERS
  (See Chapter IX—*Caveat Emptor: Chant of the Credit Gougers*)

- HOW LOAN SHARKS OPERATE
  (See Chapter X—*The Shark Has Pearly Teeth*)

- WHY THE DEBT MERCHANTS NOW WANT YOU TO BUY "PEACE OF MIND"
  (See Chapter XI—*The Peace of Mind Boom*)

- WHY AUTO DEALERS *DON'T* WANT TO SELL YOU YOUR CAR FOR CASH
  (See Chapter XII—*The Car You Buy Is Not Your Own*)

- HOW YOUR CHILDREN CAN ATTEND COLLEGE ON TIME
  (See Chapter XIII—*A Summing Up*)

BUY NOW, PAY LATER

Other books by the author

The Thief in The White Collar (*with Norman Jaspan*) 1960
The Royal Vultures (*with Sam Kolman*) 1958

332.743
B641.b

BUY NOW, PAY LATER

Hillel Black

WILLIAM MORROW AND COMPANY

NEW YORK : 1961

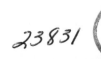
23831

TABOR COLLEGE
LIBRARY
HILLSBORO, KANSAS

Copyright © 1961 by Hillel Black
All rights reserved.
Published simultaneously in the Dominion of
Canada by George J. McLeod Limited, Toronto.
Printed in the United States of America.
Library of Congress Catalog Card Number 61-11209

Second Printing , May 1961

For Miriam and David

Preface

Until now the subject of consumer debt has been for the most part reserved for textbooks written and usually read only by economists. This report, however, is neither a volume couched in academic language nor a textbook. Frankly, I would be incapable of writing either since I am not an economist. My training is essentially reportorial. As a reporter, my concern is to investigate in human terms the breadth and meaning of debt living, what it is doing to all of us in concert, and how it affects our individual lives and the lives of our children.

To describe this phenomenon, as I believe it should be done, I explored the theories of the academician and the more immediate reality of the debt sellers and buyers. This meant going down to the market place and talking and corresponding with hundreds of people from every section of the country. My research involved pouring through seemingly endless government reports, newspapers, historical heirlooms and current business and consumer magazines as well as the testimony heard by two United States Senate subcommittees. One was the Banking and Currency subcommittee which held hearings on a consumer credit labeling bill. The other was the Judiciary subcommittee which investigated auto financing. It was only when this work was finished that I felt prepared to tell the story of America's latest and perhaps most far reaching economic and social revolution, the consumer credit explosion.

I take full responsibility for the opinions and interpretations that I have expressed in this book, though many of the conclusions and opinions concur with those drawn by others. These conclusions are the result of a concerted attempt to collect and view the facts within the limits of my own frailty and human objectivity. Finally, I must claim responsibility for the order in which the facts are presented and the questions which I have raised and tried to answer.

I would like to acknowledge the help of the following people for the time, guidance and information which they so freely and kindly gave: Dr. Ernst A. Dauer, Director of Consumer Credit Studies, Household Finance Corporation; Dr. M. R. Neifeld, Vice President of Beneficial Management Corporation; Norman Stein; Rudolph Severa; Mrs. Mildred Brady of Consumers Union; Dr. Persia Campbell; Matty Simmons, Vice President of the Diners' Club; Sidney Blitz, Education and Research Director of the New York State Credit Union League; J. Andrew Painter, Vice President First National City Bank of New York; Linn K. Twinem, Editor Personal Finance Law Quarterly Report; Mr. and Mrs. Theodore Baker of the East Harlem Protestant Parish; W. Marvin Draper, Jr. of the California Credit Union League; Mrs. Mary Jean McGrath and Warren P. Lutey of the Credit Union National Association; Richard Y. Giles, Editor of the Credit Union Bridge; Atty. Guy Sparks, Executive Assistant of the Legal Division of the Alabama Department of Revenue; Jerome Grubin; Milton R. Moskowitz; William L. Wilson, Vice President of Commercial Investment Trust Incorporated; William H. Blake, Executive Vice President of National Retail Credit Association; Martin H. Bowerman, Publications Director of Associated Credit Bureaus of America; Mrs. Helen Ewing Nelson, California Consumer Counsel; Glenn Addington, Public Relations director of the Texas Credit Union League; Mr. and Mrs. Alan Shapiro, Harry Schaudt of the Chicago Daily News.

I also wish to thank Lawrence Hughes of William Morrow & Co. for his wise editorial help and judgment, Miss Elizabeth Otis for her grace and kindness, Louise Fisher for her consideration and excellent typing, and Miriam, my wife, who makes writing and living a joy.

HILLEL BLACK

Contents

Introduction

Buy Now, Pay Later is a most illuminating and informative account of current consumer credit practices. The revelations of the interworkings of consumer debt financing to be found in this book are interesting and enjoyable reading. But they are also very serious business.

Today, personal debt is edging close to $200 billion; mortgage debt is approximately $140 billion, and consumer credit is about $55 billion. The book performs a vital public service by helping to unravel for the average American consumer some of the intricacies of this modern credit Wonderland.

Various devices are used to conceal from the consumer just what he is required to pay. Department stores ordinarily provide credit at the rate of 1½ per cent per month, which works out at about 18 per cent per year. The financing of an automobile will cost the consumer at least 12 per cent. Often it is very much more. But he ordinarily thinks he is getting credit at an interest rate of 5 or 6 per cent. Small loan companies, with stated charges of two to three per cent per month, are actually receiving from 24 to 36 per cent. The "add-on" or "discount" methods used by commercial banks make the effective rate of interest nearly double that which the consumer or borrower believes he is paying.

Last year in the United States Senate the Subcommittee on Production and Stabilization of the Senate Banking and Currency Committee, of which I am Chairman, held hearings on my bill to require full disclosure by lenders of the true cost of consumer credit. I am delighted that Mr. Black, on the basis of his careful study of this industry, states that this legislation is vital if the consumer's interest is to be protected.

The bill requires two simple pieces of information from those who are in the business of lending credit: first, the total dollar amounts of the cost of the money and, second, the expression of this amount as a true annual interest rate.

The bill does not control credit. All it asks is that the consumer be told the truth. The reduction of consumer credit financing charges to a common standard or yardstick will enable every borrower to shop around for credit as he now shops for the best trade-in for his old car or the lowest price for a new one. It would also help him to decide whether it would not be wiser for him to draw down on his savings account, on which he is receiving three or four per cent interest, rather than to finance a new purchase through consumer credit which might well cost him 12, 18, 24, or 36 per cent interest or more.

A number of objections were raised about the bill. It was said that such truthful information would merely "confuse" the consumer. We were told that "states' rights" would be offended. But even the opponents found it very difficult indeed to bring forward valid objections, for they could hardly oppose in any serious way merely giving the consumer the truth, which was all this bill called for. Mr. Black's book supplies the evidence and examples which prove the need for such a truth-in-interest bill.

Consumers do get accurate information on some types of transactions. As a *saver* in a credit union, commercial bank, or savings and loan association, the dividend and interest rates are stated in terms of the true annual rate. But when the same person buys on the installment rate or commonly borrows on personal credit, the rate is more often than not expressed in a quite different way which obscures the true interest rate.

As a borrower from most credit unions, the consumer does receive the true interest rate. As a home owner his interest rate on a mortgage is quoted as a true annual rate. If he reads the financial pages he sees that the price of credit extended to business firms is invariably quoted in terms of simple annual interest rates.

Yet, as an installment borrower or buyer the average consumer is usually denied such accurate credit-price information—information which a business man demands in order to make intelligent decisions.

My bill merely asks that the consumer be afforded the same information in the same terms as the wholesaler or retailer of credit demands for himself when he seeks to borrow money.

We live in a world in which our children can compute and recite the batting averages of their favorite ball players. Young university graduates are well versed in the complex mathematics of inter-space flight. Yet the great majority of our citizens are unaware of or are unable to decipher the rates of interest they are charged with respect to ordinary consumer credit transactions. In fact, too often the average borrower does not even receive the necessary information from the lender to be able to perform the simple arithmetic involved in determining the true annual interest rate on credit transactions.

Buy Now, Pay Later, drawing on the hearings of our Committee and the personal research of the author, can help both to inform the public and to create the climate in which reform legislation can pass.

All we ask is that the consumer be told the truth. Mr. Black clearly demonstrates the great need for the "truth-in-interest" bill.

PAUL H. DOUGLAS

March, 1961

BUY NOW, PAY LATER

1 *Enter the Debt Merchants*

Further, everything that I now possess or shall acquire is herewith pledged to Nokhutes until I shall have discharged my debt in full. Further, if Nokhutes brings suit against me for failing to meet my obligation, I admit additional liability for my damages. Further, the agent of Nokhutes is hereby authorized to deal with me, and I promise to follow his instructions unreservedly and promptly at all times.

Excerpt from a debtor's promissory note signed by a peasant slave in Thebes in 198 B.C.

As Ralph Homer placed his wallet on the night table, he reflected on the good life. He was blessed with a lovely wife and two fine children. A rising young executive employed by a growing company, he had just moved his family into a new Cape Cod House. Though the future was understandably vague, Ralph Homer was secure in his belief that nothing but the best would happen. It seemed that he had every reason to be a man contented. Take today as an example. It had been, as he had remarked to his wife Alice, one of those complete, well spent days. Indeed it had.

The day began when Ralph drove downtown to work. He had stopped at a service station to buy gasoline. Ralph discovered his wallet was empty, but paid the $3.40 with his petroleum credit card. At noon Ralph met Alice in the office lobby. Their first stop was an elegant restaurant. Lunch including drinks and tip cost $15.80. Ralph paid the bill with his all-purpose credit card.

Ever since they had moved to the suburbs Alice had been complaining that they needed a second car. So after lunch the Homers dropped in on an auto dealer. They had seen an ad in the Sunday paper offering one of those new "compacts" for no money down and thirty-six months to pay. The salesman told Ralph the car would cost him only $63.50 a month. Ralph decided he could manage the payments and signed the sales contract with no more than a glance before returning to work.

Alice planned to spend the remainder of the afternoon shopping. She carried no cash. Instead, her handbag contained a half-dozen bank charge-it cards and charga-plates. She also had four pocketbook-size directories which listed all the stores she could shop at without cash.

At a little after five Alice met Ralph at the garage near the office. She wore the smile of a triumphant woman. She had just bought a $90 dress for $59.95, a pair of $42 blue suede shoes for $29.50 and a $39 smoking jacket (for Ralph's birthday) for $28. The way Alice figured it, her bargain hunting had saved the Homer household $53.55. In reality, she had just added $117.45 to the Homer debt. But neither Ralph nor Alice would be aware of it immediately. Various revolving credit plans through which Alice made her purchases meant that the Homers would be paying only $9.78 a month for the next year. Of course, they would also be paying 18 per cent true annual interest on the declining balance. But Alice and Ralph never calculated finance charges, service charges or interest.

When Ralph started the car, he noticed a slip of paper on the windshield. It was a reminder that the garage bill was overdue. Although neither Ralph nor Alice had any money with them, Ralph decided to pay the bill—it came to $30—

with an *Instant Money* check. The Homers did not possess any of the usual checking accounts since they no longer could afford to maintain even a minimal balance. But they did have an *Instant Money* check book with which they could write almost as many checks as they wanted and then pay back the amounts of the checks in monthly installments. It was the same as borrowing money without going to the bank. Ralph made out an *Instant Money* check for $50, which not only paid the garage bill but gave him $20 in cash.

As the Homers returned in their still-to-be-paid-for car to their mortgaged home with its still-to-be-paid-for washer, dryer and living room furniture, they might have considered the fact, that already weighed down with debts, they had increased their obligations by $2472.65. They had not only managed seven transactions without exchanging a penny of cash but had ended the day with twenty dollars "more" than they had started with. If you had asked them about the state of their finances, they would have told you that theirs is an expertly managed, intelligently budgeted family. All of which was true the day the Homers married. But it wasn't long before they began building their nest on credit. And as their hopes and needs expanded, so did their debts. Today, the Homers' future is pinned to the salary Ralph has yet to make. As a homeowner and a man who has so far paid his bills, he has no trouble obtaining more debt. Now, six years after Ralph and Alice's marriage, the Homers not only have no liquid assets but have mortgaged their future for years to come. In effect, they are practicing a sort of family financial brinkmanship. Perhaps what is most disturbing is that they do not even know it.

Although the Homers are a fictitious couple, their values, spending habits, indeed their very existence are reflected in the lives of millions of American families. They have been caught in the on-the-cuff mania, the go-now, buy-now, live-now, pay-later craze. Already overloaded with debt, they are being sold even larger amounts of credit. And as the sums they owe increase, so do the opportunities for acquiring more debt.

Currently about one hundred million Americans are participating in the buy-now, pay-later binge. Furthermore, they can, if they wish, do anything and everything on credit. Babies are being born on the installment plan, children go through college on time, even funerals are being paid for on what the English quaintly call "the never never." Through debt people are buying hairpins, toothpaste, mink coats, girdles, tickets to baseball games, religious medallions, hi-fi equipment, safaris in Africa. Most of these items were sold for the first time on *time* only during the last decade. For example, half of all the furniture, TV sets, washing machines and outboard motorboats are bought on *time,* in addition to two-thirds of all new cars. The result has been a consumer credit explosion that makes the population explosion seem small by comparison.

The enormous force of this explosion can be measured by these figures. All consumer debt, that is debt owed by individuals as distinguished from business or the government, totals a staggering $195 billion, nearly a 200 per cent increase over the past ten years. In the same period consumer's disposable income increased only 60 per cent. A breakdown shows that Americans currently owe $139 billion in home mortgages and $56 billion in intermediate and short term debt, or what the Federal Government calls "consumer credit." This $56 billion debt includes money owed on cars, appliances, home repairs, small loans, charge accounts, revolving credit and credit cards. Consumer credit—the key to the rise in private debt—has increased over 550 per cent since 1940. In the last ten years it has more than doubled. By 1970 experts predict consumer credit will reach $107 billion, or nearly double again.

And how is all this credit being paid for? The money comes not only out of people's current but also future earnings. As we enter the nineteen sixties the American people must work over two months out of twelve to reimburse their creditors. In an alarming number of instances, however, people find that no matter how hard or how long they labor they can't meet their debts. The result has been a sharp increase in family bankruptcies. During the fiscal year of 1959 nearly 89,000 families failed financially, a 300 per cent increase over the past decade and more than the total number of bankruptcies filed during the height of the Depression. These families represented 88.3 per cent of all failures filed under the United States Bankruptcy Act and that includes all business, farm and professional bankruptcies. Thousands of others avoid failure by the expeditious means of extending the number of payment periods, which only puts them deeper into debt. According to the statisticians the average American family is only three months away from financial failure.

Being in debt is not new. The Babylonians, the Egyptians, the Celts and the Romans among other civilizations, extended credit. Even the Puritans on the Mayflower bought passage on an installment plan. However, in mid-century America, as the result of the consumer credit explosion, the total private debt is certainly greater than the combined private debt of man throughout history. Never have so many owed so much. Never has so much profit been made out of debt itself. To conceive of how much credit costs the American consumer, one need just estimate the interest paid a year. It comes to over eleven billion dollars, a conservative guess. This is nearly half again as much as the public pays through the tax collector on the mammoth debt of the Federal Government. And it is twice as much as the total expenditures of the Federal Government from the administration of George Washington through the first term of Woodrow Wilson.

Companion with the consumer credit explosion has been the emergence of a new type of entrepreneur, the debt merchant. Although people throughout the ages have made profit through the sale of debt, this is the first time that debt merchandising has been conducted on such a gigantic scale. Today, every auto dealer, commercial bank, department store, small loan operator, sales finance company, as well as nearly every Main Street retailer is in the business of selling debt.

This book will describe that industry and how it operates. It will also explore what debt living is doing to people in the United States, the disturbing strains and tragedies that can result from keeping up with the bill collector and the continued warping of our values where the possession of goods becomes all-consuming. Finally, this report will examine the values of the debt merchants themselves. It will show how in too many instances morality has left the market place, that the consumer and the consumer's children are being sold debt with what often appears to be the cynical abandon of a carnival huckster.

Perhaps the best introduction to the extent of consumer debt can be summed up in the experience of Joseph Miraglia, a nineteen-year-old clerk from New York's Lower East Side.

Joe had spotted a stack of credit card applications in a

restaurant. He sent one in, and a few weeks later received a big white envelope with a Carte Blanche card inside. Card in hand and a wallet full of dreams, Joe checked into a $55 suite in the Waldorf-Astoria Hotel in New York. During the succeeding weeks he was to dine and sport in the fanciest hotels and nightclubs in Montreal, Miami, Havana and Las Vegas. A $73-a-week clerk, he had no trouble in purchasing on credit a $675 silver mink stole for a girl friend, a $35 cocker spaniel which he fed filet mignon dinners, and two thousand dollars worth of clothes including five pairs of shoes and eight custom-made silk shirts. The total cost of his adventure came to ten thousand dollars. Shortly after Joe Miraglia was caught, he explained how it happened: "All the Carte Blanche application said was that it would open a new and magical world to me. Other ads seemed to grow out of every corner of the city saying you should go now, pay later—live it up and charge it. I couldn't believe it was as easy as that, but I wanted to find out."

2 The Rub in Aladdin's Lamp

YOU CAN HAVE CULTURE ON CREDIT TOO.
Thanks to a contract between the American Ballet
Theatre and The Diners' Club . . .

From Diners' Club Magazine, *circulation
more than one million.*

Not long ago an American newspaperman was dining at a night club in Madrid when his eye was captivated by the establishment's dancing girl. The newspaperman asked the headwaiter whether the night club could part with the dancer's services for the remainder of the evening. The headwaiter agreed, providing señor paid for her time. As the American started to write out a personal check, the headwaiter shook his head. He could not accept credit in such a form from a stranger. The American then drew out his Diners' Club card. The headwaiter needed to see no more. He took out his pencil and proceeded to charge the lady as dessert.

Although the Spanish trifle has yet to be listed in Diners' official directory, you as a card holder may charge nearly anything else almost anywhere in the world. Simply by paying six dollars apiece you can enjoy all the privileges offered by one of the Big Three—American Express, Carte Blanche or Diners' Club.* Depending upon the card you hold, you may do the following: dine at Maxim's in Paris; hire an African safari; take a Turkish bath in Tokyo; put up your horse at a Las Vegas horse motel where the oats are free; hunt polar bear in Alaska and, if you outsmart the bear, have it stuffed by an Alaskan taxidermist. You may also buy a Lilly Daché hat, rent a Hertz car, stop at the Hilton Hotel in Cairo, the Ritz Hotel in Bombay or visit Frankie's Band Box in Pittsburgh. You can buy blouses at Bartolini's in Florence, convention cigars that say Mazel Tov, live Maine lobsters by the peck, or make your purchase at a Tokyo store with a sign in the window that reads: "Diners' Club spoken here." You can also charge candy, cocktails, deodorants, and salami. And if you're concerned about how you will pay for all this when you are billed thirty days later, you might take a chance by starting a game currently in vogue among a group of Los Angeles businessmen. They are playing a luncheon "Russian roulette" with credit cards. Everyone puts his card face down in the middle of the table and the waiter blindly selects the one to pay the tab.

The possibility that more of us may yet turn to the Los Angeles form of gamesmanship is indeed likely considering the amount of goods and services purchased with the all-purpose credit card. By the beginning of 1960, the munificent sum of nearly four hundred million dollars was charged through the Big Three. That yearly figure should easily surpass the half-billion dollar mark by the end of 1961. At the start of 1960, Diners', American Express and Carte

---

* Diners' and American Express have held intermittent discussions for over a year on a possible merger. Talks were still continuing at this writing.

Blanche had over two million dues-paying, card-carrying members. Before the next few years have passed that figure probably will double.

Typical of the consumer credit explosion, the growth of the all-purpose credit card has been phenomenal. Its portent, though, for the future may mean a decided crimp in the American family's pocketbook. And this may be true even though expenditure through credit cards is only a drop in the vat of consumer debt, a hefty fifty-six billion dollars in 1960. But before exploring the future of the universal credit card industry, it would be worthwhile to examine how it got started and why it succeeded. The story may well be entitled: "How I Turned One of Life's Embarrassing Moments into a Million Dollar Business."

It all began one February night in 1950, when a struggling New Yorker, Frank MacNamara, decided to work late at his office, the Hamilton Credit Company. MacNamara, a thirty-five-year-old specialist in commercial credit, took time off to have dinner at a strange restaurant. Upon presentation of the bill, MacNamara discovered he had misplaced his wallet. Faced with the possibility that he might have to spend the rest of the evening among the restaurant's pots and pans, he put in a hasty call to his wife on Long Island to bail him out. She arrived two hours later with the money. The next day MacNamara had lunch with his lawyer, Ralph Schneider. As MacNamara recounted his experiences, the two hatched the idea of what was to become The Diners' Club. In the credit card industry, MacNamara's dinner is now fondly referred to as The First Supper.

As soft-spoken Ralph Schneider was to tell me a decade later in his sumptuous offices on the tenth floor of New York's Coliseum: "Both MacNamara and I solicited business.

It was rough sledding. Plenty of skepticism on the part of the establishments. They just didn't think it would work. They were concerned about the concentration of charges. I guess they didn't believe we would take the risk of giving the customer a blank check. There was also skepticism on the part of the card holders. Just by applying they would get the credit card and we would take the risk. They thought there had to be a catch."

During the first week MacNamara and Schneider canvassed ten New York restaurants. The response was negative. But by the end of the third week a dozen restaurants had joined, forming the nucleus for what was to become a worldwide multicellular operation. They signed up one hundred card carriers by mailing a prospectus to five thousand sales managers. In the meantime they set up an office with a girl to take care of the bookkeeping and hired ebullient, cigar-smoking Matty Simmons, a night club and restaurant publicity man who is now a Diners' vice president. MacNamara and Schneider worked Simmons' contacts as well as their own and the list of restaurants and cardholders began to grow. By the end of the second year MacNamara and Schneider plunged over $58,000 into debt. But goods and services charged with the Diners' credit card came to over one million dollars. After that, Diners' was always to make a profit. By March 31, 1960, Diners had total billings of $165 million. The total profit for that year, nearly two million dollars. A starveling only a decade ago, the Diners' Club has developed a corporate pot that is the envy of many a businessman.

One man not destined to share fully in these riches was Frank MacNamara. He sold out his interests to Board Chairman Schneider and Alfred Bloomingdale, now president, for $200,000. MacNamara had wanted Diners' to go into the mail-order business. Schneider then preferred sticking to credit cards. In 1957, four years after he sold out, Mac-Namara died. Recently the club started selling via mail order, marketing vitamin pills for Diners' members.

Both Schneider and Bloomingdale have become million-aires. During the winter the board chairman commutes be-tween his home in the Virgin Islands and his eight-room co-operative apartment in the Hotel Pierre in New York. When not flying south, he may relax by playing cards, or immersing himself in the steam bath at New York's boatless Lone Star Boat Club.

Schneider, whose initial investment was only ten thousand dollars, still is afflicted with moments of disbelief when he contemplates Diners' and his success. Recently *The Wall Street Journal* devoted a full-length feature article to Schnei-der in its Road to Riches series. Diners' chief executive told a *Journal* reporter how he landed a clerk's job in a law office in 1932. His salary was then five dollars a week. "Someone asked," he relates, "whether any of us would settle for a guaranteed wage of one hundred dollars a week for life if he knew he would never earn anything less, and never any-thing more. I was one of those who said he would take it. I'm very lucky nobody made me the offer."

Although the Diners' Club is the oldest, the largest and the most successful among the all-purpose credit cards, it is actually a late comer to the credit-card field. The first known credit card offered the American public wasn't really a credit card but a letter of credit. Called the "Traveletter System," it was introduced in 1894 and used by executives and salesmen so that they could charge traveling and lodging expenses. It wasn't until the nineteen thirties that the credit card itself really came into its own. The petroleum industry began offering credit cards which would be honored by service stations for the purchase of gasoline. Today there are forty-nine million such cards in existence, with an estimated four billion dollars charged annually.

As you may imagine, keeping track of forty-nine million cards is a series of myriad operations. Typical are the Midwest credit card offices of Standard of Indiana with 357 employees who work two eight-hour shifts five days a week. They keep track of one and one-half million card holders in twelve states and are forced to use so much automated equipment that the Chicago offices look like the control room at Cape Canaveral. The intricacies of the operation may be gleaned from just this one example. Standard's Midwest headquarters receives between 150,000 and 300,000 sales tickets from dealers each day. Every sales ticket is put on microfilm and stored for safekeeping in the hills of Wisconsin. The purpose of this operation is to keep a permanent record of all bills in case of a catastrophe like the explosion of a hydrogen bomb. Only a dozen or so motorists may survive. One or two, though, may still have outstanding charges. It is an axiom in the credit industry that nobody takes a chance of missing a collection.

Despite the huge billing expense, the petroleum industry thinks credit cards are worth-while. According to a survey conducted by du Pont, gasoline credit cards, which incidentally are free, are owned by 12 per cent of the nation's motorists. A little more than half of all petroleum-card owners also charge tires, batteries and minor services. The chance is slim that the petroleum industry will ever accept a universal gasoline card. Each company issues its own card to insure brand loyalty. And brand loyality is too juicy a plum to share.

Besides the forty-nine million petroleum cards, there are eight million other credit cards in existence, including three million equally divided between the Bank of America and American Telephone and Telegraph. The phone company's cardholders yearly charge more than fifty million calls costing more than eighty million dollars. Another 800,000 have been issued by the Universal Air Travel Plan which allows its holders to charge plane rides after they have plunked down an initial deposit of $425. You can add another 250,000 cards which are good on fifty-seven railroads. The remainder belong to the all-purpose credit card enterprises, numerous banking plans, department stores and a various host of smaller operations including one called Cruise Clubs, Inc. This card allows over 2,500 yachtsmen to put in at any one of 6,038 ports and charge for marine, gas, dockage fees, servicing and harbor motels. Practically the only item you can't charge on a credit card is a funeral payment. In fact, Diners' has already turned down a die-now pay-later plan. Apparently no one was able to answer the question: How do you collect from the hereafter?

In this land of ours where time buying has become a way of life, the future of the credit card industry would appear almost limitless. Adding up the total number of credit cards in existence we reach the grand total of fifty-seven million, and that is probably a conservative figure. By the end of 1960 there were approximately sixty-four million families in the United States. Soon there will be at least one credit card outstanding for every family in America. Of course, not every family owns a credit card. In fact, some people own a score

or more. And that, in part, is one of the reasons why Diners'
has been so successful. If you were a charge-it addict before
Diners' blossomed, your credit card collection was as unwieldy as a canasta deck. Diners'—which has witnessed or
joined in the burial of twenty-one other companies—and its
current competitors are attempting to end the confusion of
the two-wallet man.

As all Diners' Club spokesmen are eager to tell you, the
practical conveniences have weighed heavily in the growth
of the organization. As they put it: "One credit card. One
monthly bill. One check to pay for all your charges." Another argument effectively used by Diners' and others is
only found in an expense account economy. By using a
credit card, you present the tax collector with an itemized
bill. What's more, neither you nor your employer has to
carry the additional bookkeeping costs. The use of credit
cards has led to even greater corner cutting in the country's
periodic venture into fraud—designing our annual income
tax returns.

On December 30, 1959, Federal Tax Commissioner Dana
Latham was forced to note in Washington: "I'm a little
afraid abuses of the federal income tax are growing." He
traced part of the difficulty to credit cards, which are used
for both business and personal expenses. He said the real
problem arose from blanket expense allowances for which
employees do not have to account. He then gave the example
of the employee who uses a credit card. The bills go direct
to the company which pays them but does not ask the employee to detail the expenditures. There is a trend, he went
on, for business to grant such unrestricted expense allowances to officers and top employees as a kind of "fringe benefit." Companies deduct all these payments as business

expenses. But the officers and employees do not report the money as additional compensation which it often is when spent for anything except strictly business reasons. Besides the obvious loss in tax revenue, Commissioner Latham observed "a deep resentment on the part of taxpayers who feel their next-door neighbors are getting a better break than they are." How all this has affected our mores may be noted in this social footnote that may even have startled Kinsey. Before the credit card era began, the traveling businessman who took along his secretary would list her as his wife. Today, he takes his wife and claims she is his secretary.

The final and perhaps most telling reason for the success of the all-purpose credit card can be summed up in one household word: status. A publicity release hailing Diners' tenth anniversary noted: "The psychology of credit cards had a great deal to do with the success of The Diners' Club. To charge is to attain a status and this has been an age of status. The businessman is striving for success and to have automatic credit wherever one goes has become a symbol of success."

The publicity man has divined a simple truth. The virtue of thrift once expounded by Benjamin Franklin has been turned into the virtue of the spendthrift. In a society where spending is becoming the ultimate value, there exists the companion phenomenon—only the needy carry cash. Ironically, the man who flourishes a bankroll is not only a boor but even his personal integrity and character are suspect. Today the man of means whips out a credit card, signs his name and no questions are asked. As all who watch him know, this man has arrived.

I offered up the phenomena of the credit card to Dr. Ernest Dichter. As president of the Institute of Motivational Research, Dr. Dichter is a recognized expert on our subterranean motives.

"In general," Dr. Dichter opined, "we have been shifting more and more from a puritanical culture to a hedonistic one. This is partly the result of economic, psychological, and political developments. We are more concerned with immediate happiness rather than counting on delayed satisfactions in life, or the life hereafter. A credit card is a symbol of this hedonistic age. We are getting our pleasures, our purchases, our entertainment, before we've actually earned them.

"The credit card," Dr. Dichter continues, "is the modern Lamp of Aladdin. All you need to do is show it, sign it, rub it and—presto—the thing you wish for appears and is yours. In many ways this is another demonstration by the human being of potency, of power. Through it we have achieved what we have always dreamed about as human beings, to control our destiny at least in the form of an illusion, yet tangible enough to be translated into products and services."

For Diners' the greatest asset the club has is an extraordinary membership of built-in status seekers. Certainly no one was more pleased than the club's top brass when it received the results of a *Diners' Club Magazine* Reader Survey in the fall of 1959. (*Diners' Club Magazine,* a monthly which goes to members, carries articles and stories by such well known authors as Ogden Nash, Garson Kanin, Irwin Shaw, Ludwig Bemelmans and Eddie Cantor. No status seeker could ask for more.)

Diners' discovered that more than 45 per cent of its members are salesmen or corporation executives. The remainder include a sprinkling of accountants, lawyers, doctors, dentists, engineers, scientists, artists, writers, public relations

23831

TABOR COLLEGE
LIBRARY
HILLSBORO, KANSAS

men and advertising executives. The smallest group of members consist of clergymen and labor union executives. Together they make up four-fifths of 1 per cent. This is the overall portrait of the average member: an executive, he is married and has 2.1 children, a college graduate, he admits to 42½ years and owns a $30,419 home. His average annual income is $16,876.35, three times the national average.

Despite the affluence of its members and increasing volume of its billings, Diners', along with Carte Blanche and American Express, is afflicted by a problem of numbers. Similar to the mass media magazines, the credit card companies can only thrive by a rabbit-like increase in their membership rolls. The basic reason is a simple economic fact of life. The credit card companies make up their operating costs through commissions paid by the establishments that honor the cards.

For example, when you charge a meal at a restaurant with a Diners' Club card, your bill is sent to Diners' headquarters. The restaurant is reimbursed by Diners'. Diners', meanwhile, deducts 7 per cent from the price of your meal, a sum the restaurant pays. This sum goes to Diners' for the handling, bookkeeping, and collection of the money the cardholder pays Diners' at the end of the thirty-day billing period. The commissions the member establishments pay vary. Diners' charges all restaurants 7 per cent. American Express between 5 and 7, and Carte Blanche offers an alluring 4 per cent. This figure, though, is based on the total check, including tips and taxes. Hotels pay between 3 and 5 per cent and specialty shops as much as 10 per cent. For the 1959-1960 fiscal year, Diners' received more than $9,700,000 in commissions. This sum just about covered Diners' operating costs, which are high. For example, the club had to pay out nearly $1,400,000 just for credit investigations and collections. Diners' profits come from the five-dollar yearly fee it charges each card holder.* The only way Diners' and its competitors can increase profits and remain popular is for Diners' and the others to enlarge their general membership.

There you have the rub in Aladdin's Lamp. If the all-purpose credit card becomes as common as the dollar bill, it is no longer a status symbol. And that is what has been happening. Generally, you must earn a minimum of $5,000 a year to join Diners' and American, and $7,500 to belong to Carte Blanche. In addition, a credit check must show that you can and do pay your bills. The only two members who received Diners' cards without such a check were Harry S. Truman and Mrs. Ivy Baker Priest, at the time United States Treasurer. Mrs. Priest was given a solid gold card as the five-hundred-thousandth member. After the presentation one of Diners' credit men asked the club's president whether a credit check was in order. Alfred Bloomingdale sent the memo to Mrs. Priest with the question: "What's your bank?" Mrs. Priest replied: "Fort Knox."

Since Mrs. Priest was given her free card, there has been a tidal wave of new joiners. This, of course, has been encouraged by Diners'. And now that Hilton has entered the field with Carte Blanche and American Express with its card, the competition among The Big Three has become a race to build ever greater rosters. It has reached the point where even children apply for membership.

Not long ago American Express received an application from a lady who listed her residence as Scarsdale, New York. Her husband, she said, was named William. The local credit officials were unable to locate anyone by the name of William.

---

* You may join Diners' for five dollars, but you must pay an additional dollar if you wish to receive the *Diners' Club Magazine*.

A further check turned up the following. The lady in the application was actually eight. She had hoped to use her credit card at her local candy store.

The drive to enlist more members pinned the credit card companies on the horns of a second dilemma. By extending the credit privileges to an ever-widening group of people eager to live on the cuff, the risk of loss mounts. Each time someone does not pay the tab he has charged with a credit card, it is not the restaurant owner or merchant who absorbs the loss but the credit card company. Texaco, for example, reports bad debts on the oil company's credit card now run about .37 per cent of charge volume, three times the percentage of a smaller volume eight years ago. Diners' reports its bad debt figures total .6 per cent of volume, or triple the rate of 1952. Although the percentage may seem small, multiply the percentage against the club's outstanding charges and the loss figure for 1959 comes to about one million dollars, equal to almost half of Diners' net profits. And Diners' is the most experienced in the field. To avoid dead beats, the club has upped its rejection rate to 40 per cent of all applications and already has turned cards down on royalty and several millionaires who refuse to pay their bills.

Despite the credit checks, the credit card companies still get hooked. One reason is that some people go on a charge-it spree with the result that their debts pile up to the point where they can no longer pay the tab. Take the case of the socially prominent family whose daughter eloped with an elevator operator. The young lady's dowry was a credit card. With it, the elevator operator was able to take his bride on a five thousand dollar honeymoon ride through Europe. It took the credit card company seven months before it could force the angry father to pay up.

Frequently, a thorough credit check will flash in advance whether a potential member will turn "sour"—a term applied by the credit industry to those who refuse to honor their time payments. One credit manager of a large Eastern oil company told me that his company offered credit-card applications to the members of two plush country clubs. Credit checks, however, resulted in a 25 per cent turn down. As the credit manager put it: "We had to turn them down. Although their average earnings were twenty thousand dollars a year, they were living on thirty thousand." The credit manager also reported similar results when his company canvassed a group of political appointees, policemen, and firemen in one of New Jersey's more populous counties. Those rejected earned an average of six thousand dollars annually. They were spending as much as nine thousand dollars.

Recently, H. M. Barrentine of Skelly Oil Company surveyed all the members of the American Petroleum Credit Association on the subject of fraud and the misuse of credit cards. His replies totaled 100 per cent. He classified the credit card abuses into these three categories. They are listed here in descending order of volume losses.

1. Cards stolen outright or misused by some member of the family.
2. Where the owner of the card suddenly went haywire.
3. Cards obtained through misrepresentation with no intent to pay.

Although the third category represents the smallest total volume loss, it usually produces the greatest losses dollar-wise, as far as individual cases are concerned. The credit-card cheat is not only growing in numbers, but has opened new vistas of fraud.

Besides a few cases of eager innocents such as Joseph Miraglia mentioned in Chapter 1, an unusual group of professional thieves has joined the American scene. Lusty and lusting for the finer things in life they have mined a world of riches with the Aladdin's Lamp of consumer credit. It has reached the point where the F.B.I. has found it necessary to create a whole new criminal category: "Most wanted credit-card thief."

One of the gamest is an elegant ex-con by the name of Charles Gregory Cannon. When taken into custody in New York by the F.B.I., Cannon sported a silver-handled cane and a broad British accent. The F.B.I. found in his hotel room a two-thousand-dollar portable printing press which he used to print his own credit cards and checks. According to Assistant United States Attorney David P. Bicks, who has handled several cases involving credit-card cheats, the dapper Cannon traveled extensively throughout the Northeast and Canada. During a five-month period, Bicks said, he cashed twenty thousand dollars in fraudulent checks and spent another twenty thousand dollars in hotels and restaurants with his phony credit cards. Though noticeably slim when arrested, Cannon somehow managed to spend twenty-five dollars nightly for dinner.

Cannon's take was small compared to a Canadian ring which set up a printing plant to duplicate credit cards issued by the Diners' Club. Although Diners' did not suffer any serious financial loss, the group, using the cards as identification, managed to pass over $250,000 in bad checks at several Canadian banks.

In contrast to those who counterfeit credit cards, a substantial business has grown up in stolen credit cards. Assistant U.S. Attorney Bicks reported the case of a six-member ring which was recently sentenced in New York. These carefree credit-card buccaneers passed more than one hundred thousand dollars in bad checks by using stolen credit cards as references. Says Bicks: "This was a national operation. They were operating as a conspiracy and they had every conceivable kind of credit card. They flew all over the country in jets, living on the cards and cashing checks on the way."

On occasion, the frenzied quest for new members has unwittingly resulted in a credit card cheat. Not long ago a resident of Minneapolis decided to investigate the contents of a trash can. His efforts were rewarded, for he came across the nearest thing to a blank check. In this instance, a Hilton Carte Blanche credit card. A short time later he landed in Chicago. Within less than eight hours the Minneapolis treasure hunter had run up bills totaling eight hundred dollars at a camera shop and at a ritzy clothing shop affiliated with the Carte Blanche plan. A clerk, however, became suspicious and phoned Carte Blanche headquarters. The Hilton people made a quick check and discovered that they had mailed the card to a man who had been dead two years. Whoever had received it, apparently had thrown it away.

How did the error happen? When Hilton climbed aboard the credit-card wagon in early 1959, they mailed out one million Carte Blanche cards to persons formerly listed by the Hilton Hotels as credit customers. Carte Blanche members are now charged a six-dollar annual fee when they use the card outside of a Hilton Hotel.

Perhaps the most disheartening problem the credit card companies face are the thieves who find eager partners among the businessmen who agree to honor the cards. *The Wall Street Journal* records the case of a former Manhattan advertising executive who managed to have a large oil company finance a leisurely jaunt through the Southwest. The former ad man owned a pink 1958 Lincoln sedan and a credit card issued by the Esso Standard Oil Division of Humble Oil & Refining Company. Among other things, he appeared to be charging tires every two weeks. Actually, he wasn't buying all those new tires. He simply persuaded the service station operators to charge them to his credit card account. Instead of taking the tires he would pocket the money the tires cost, kicking back a percentage to the co-operative operator. By the end of his journey, the ad man had managed to run up a three thousand dollar bill, which Esso had to charge off. As an Esso credit official said, "This is the kind of thing that makes the credit card business a little discouraging."

The Diners' Club had an even more discouraging experience during the 1959 season at Miami Beach. A stolen credit card ring, which worked the Beach's B-girl joints, managed to run up between seventy-five thousand and one hundred thousand dollars in fraudulent sales. According to Philip Adelman, a Diners' official, the ring used waiters to steal the cards. The waiters would pick the customers' pockets and in several instances gave the customers knockout drops so that they could pick their billfolds. The ring also employed merchants, restaurant owners and night club operators. One pizza parlor, for example, charged a phony customer five hundred dollars. A Chinese restaurant charged another seven hundred dollars. And one night club used a stolen credit card to bill a customer five hundred dollars and then added another four hundred for a tip. Diners', of course, no longer does business with these Miami Beach establishments. As Adelman noted: "It has always been the policy of Diners' to pay off merchants who unknowingly sell goods to a person with a stolen credit card. We absorb the loss and we will continue to do so unless the charges are obviously and flagrantly false."

To keep the bloodletting at a minimum, the all-purpose credit card companies have instituted several discreet safeguards of which most of their members are not aware. The maximum amount each cardholder can charge without approval generally runs around one hundred dollars. Just before the 1959 Christmas season, Hilton slashed its maximum allowance from five hundred to one hundred dollars. If the customer wants to charge more than one hundred dollars, the merchant usually is supposed to obtain approval by calling central headquarters collect. American Express has one department that works around the clock seven days a week taking calls from all over the country. In addition, twenty clerks at American Express daily check each of the thousands of charge slips that pour into the office. Each cardholder is rated according to his credit risk. The clerks add each incoming charge to his account. If the customer surpasses his individual debt limit, the account is then turned over to a supervisor for study.

Credit-card companies also work up confidential blacklists of people who buy now, but never pay. These lists identify cards that have either been stolen or lost. The blacklists are sent to all member establishments. Diners' lists usually contain about two hundred names. However, American Express has sent out a list with eighteen hundred names and Carte Blanche had one list that included thirty-five hundred dead beats, skips and lost or stolen cards. When the lists become that unwieldy, they may prove no help. A salesman or cashier may either be too lazy or too busy to check the names.

Incidentally, if you are a credit cardholder and the card is lost or stolen, report the loss immediately to the company. Unless the loss has been reported, you will be held responsible for all charges made on your card. The safest procedure is to phone or wire the credit card office, then send a registered letter.

Several credit-card companies actually have men whose full-time job is to pick up cards that have been declared invalid. Diners' has a staff of twelve. American Express can call on its own staff of detectives who until recently spent the major part of their time protecting the company's Travelers Cheques. Headed by a former F.B.I. man, these company sleuths have been responsible for the jailing of some of the nation's most notorious thieves.

The abuse that followed the current popularity of credit cards has resulted in a series of laws that would have been unheard of only ten years ago. At least four states—Texas, Florida, Georgia and Kentucky—have enacted legislation aimed at curbing credit-card thieves. The first and so far the toughest was passed in Texas in May, 1959. Maximum penalties for the misuse of a credit card include a ten thousand dollar fine and ten years in jail. It is expected that within the next decade the majority of states will enact legislation similar to, though perhaps not as stringent as, the Texas law. Among other original contributions, it appears that credit cards are opening a whole new field of criminal jurisprudence.

A question that still must be answered: will universal credit cards mean higher prices for both card holders and cash payers? Here are some facts from which there can be little relief. Roughly 80 per cent of all credit-card charges are made in restaurants. This means each time a meal is charged from 4 to 7 per cent is deducted from the restaurants owner's pocket. Who will make up the difference? The restaurant owner or the consumer? That problem is rocking the restaurant world as no other. For the gastronomic specialist, the battle of the charge-it buffet has left a bitter taste.

During the spring of 1959, restaurants in Cleveland, Portland, Oregon, and Seattle revolted against the commissions they had to pay to partake of the credit-card pie. Said the restaurants: "We simply can't afford to charge the prices we do when the credit-card companies take such a terrific bite out of our profits." One restaurant owner tried to beat the system by charging his credit-card customers a 5 per cent surcharge. This time, though, the customers revolted.

The credit-card companies are quick to contend that instead of being squeezed the restaurants are developing a bulge from on-the-cuff diners. Not only are more people eating out, but they spend more. A series of surveys tend to bear out the credit-card companies' claims. *Restaurant Management,* the magazine for the restaurant trade, had its entire editorial staff devote ten months to the study of credit cards. The magazine noted: "In the great majority of restaurants surveyed by our staff, operators stated that credit cards had brought in additional business." The average estimates ranged from seventeen additional customers per week in Boston to thirty-five in Baltimore and much higher figures in cities such as New York.

The trade publication goes on to say: "The answer to how this 'plus' business is brought in is simple when one realizes that up to a million people may be carrying the name of a restaurant around in their pockets. The name, of course, is in the credit-card directory, and it is to this directory members turn when visiting another city or even when looking for a new restaurant in their own town."

Even more startling is the claim that a man using his credit card will spend as much as 25 to 30 per cent more simply because he has not paid cash. Says *Restaurant Management:* "When we talk about top-volume operators with a changing and growing clientele, the average check that is charged through a major credit-card company will be from 20 to 25 per cent higher. *Life,* in an article on credit cards, put the figure higher (25 to 35 per cent). These figures are not theoretical but are based on survey after survey."

This impulse buying has been explained as the result of the "inexhaustible potency" a man feels when he is armed with a credit card. Others have offered the simpler dictum: "Man, I'm living now. Who cares what I have to pay later." Whatever the explanation, it appears that a gourmet, possessed by his credit card, can turn into a glutton.

But no matter how many bulging forty's and bay windows credit cards produce, there seems to be little doubt that Mr. and Mrs. Consumer will have to pay more for the things they buy and for dining out. Just ten years ago 95 per cent of all restaurants could refuse credit to their customers and get by. Today only 25 to 30 per cent of the larger-volume restaurants can still close their cash registers to some form of credit. As *Restaurant Management* put it: "Credit cards and the credit way of life are here to stay."

When the problem was posed to Donald Greenaway, executive vice president of the National Restaurant Association, he noted that the average profit in the restaurant industry is only 3 or 3½ per cent. "Much too small," he said, "to pay five or seven per cent commission on this growing volume of credit business."

"If its present growth continues," Greenaway went on, "the credit card is bound to affect most forms of retail business. What will happen is simple: Someone must pay the cost of the credit service. Inevitably, it's going to be the customer —the cash customer as well as the credit customer. The cost will be paid in the form of higher prices. If the American consumer is going to demand ever-increasing credit—and it appears he is—the American consumer must pay for his credit, visibly or invisibly."

Restaurant Management was equally candid. Concluding its thirty-page report, the magazine said: "The last thing is that, ultimately, the customer will have to be the one who pays. He will not do this through an increase in his yearly charge from the credit-card companies, but through increased restaurant prices. Some operators predict that this will be disastrous to the restaurant industry. *We sincerely doubt that the customer will even notice—particularly the credit-card customer.*" (Italics added.)

Is there an answer? A travel agent by the name of L. B. Rozee thought he had one when in 1958 he started the Rozee Bonus Card Club with headquarters in New York. A credit-card club in reverse, members pay five dollars to join and receive a 10 per cent discount if they pay cash. According to J. W. Kaufman, the club's new president—Rozee sold out in late 1959—some twenty-seven hundred motels, hotels and restaurants in the United States and Canada honor the card. "When this nightmare of credit blows up," said Kaufman, "we'll probably be bigger than The Diners' Club." It would seem, though, that the Rozee Bonus Card Club—it continues to bear the Rozee name—has some way to go before it even qualifies as a gadfly. In May, 1959, Rozee claimed twenty-five thousand members. When I talked to Kaufman over a year later, he said the figure hadn't changed and that a number of the cards were not paid for.

It appears that credit cards and the all-purpose cards in particular are rooted in our way of life as surely as apple pie, Marilyn Monroe and slaughter on the highways. Perhaps the story that most dramatically shows how popular credit cards have become is the success that Diners' has had not just in the United States, but throughout almost the entire world. Starting in 1953, Diners' managed to set up more than forty-eight franchises which cover more than one hundred countries and territories. This means that not only Americans may hold credit cards but so may the citizens of Argentina, the Congo, Tahiti, Surinam and Zanzibar, to name only a few. What is perhaps even more remarkable is that Diners' has sold the American passion for credit to cultures that held that the man who bought on time was both one step away from poverty and two steps ahead of the law. As I listened to M. Mark Sulkes, the exuberant and eloquent head of Diners' international operations, explain what he and his staff had accomplished, I somehow felt the time would come when all over the globe the man of means appearing without his all-purpose credit card would be a man unclothed.

"Credit," said M. Mark Sulkes, "is an act of faith. And what is the basic form of credit? The bank check. Yet in Europe it was not unusual to see runners with bags chained to their wrists. The bags contained cash. For many people, including large utility companies, would not accept checks. It was our job to explain that a person who uses credit is a man of substance. It took us seven years. Today we have over one hundred thousand Diners' members in Europe alone. And another eighty thousand in other foreign countries."

One of Sulkes' major accomplishments was to crack the Iron Curtain, where he worked out an arrangement to have Diners' cards honored in Yugoslavia. When I saw him, he was negotiating with Bulgaria and working on a plan to have Diners' accepted by Intourist in Russia. This would obviate all exchange of money. For M. Mark Sulkes faith in credit has become a crusade.

But how, I wondered, did Diners' ever become acceptable in Western Europe, let alone the East? Part of Sulkes' success can be explained by a million-dollar promotion campaign which Diners' used to make joiners out of doubters. In addition, Sulkes himself travels some 30,000 miles a year and has visited some sixty countries on his credit crusade. Wherever Sulkes or his colleagues went there would be cocktail parties, press conferences, speeches, a veritable paean to on-the-cuff living and what it could do for hotels, restaurants and shops of other lands. The most successful selling gimmick was Sulkes' plan in 1957 to send a couple around the world without a farthing in their pockets. The lucky couple, Mr. and Mrs. Harold A. Bortzfield, won the trip on a TV show, *The Big Program*. They went from New York to New York. Their entire treasury consisted of a Diners' Club card.

"In West Germany alone," Sulkes recalls, "there were forty-two front-page articles describing the Bortzfields' trip. Wherever they went they were badgered by newspaper people, television, radio. In Paris, they were met by the mayor. And, of course, each time they explained what the Diners' Club does."

Sulkes' campaign was so successful that by the spring of 1960, there were over eighteen thousand foreign establishments that honor a Diners' Club card. This may end the international Babel of money which confronts the neophyte traveler. For the Diners' card holder it works this way. When an Italian member goes to Brazil, all he must do is present his Diners' card. The Brazilian Diners' Club then bills the

Italian Diners' Club which pays in Brazilian coin or American dollars.

Perhaps Sulkes' greatest triumph took place in Spain. "Spain, as you know," he says, "has a very poor population. Only the top Spanish noble families, the titled gentry, the top bankers, and businessmen have any wealth. Before we came to Spain the idea of credit as we know it was nonexistent. There, if a rich man went to a tailor, he would order several suits and then wait as long as two years before he would pay his bill. If a noble went into a restaurant, the waiter would bow and scrape, but would never dare present a bill. Maybe six months later the manager would call the noble and prayerfully beg for his money. Today, we have six thousand members in Spain, nearly every wealthy Spaniard in the country. And how, you ask, did we get these people to pay their Diners' bill on time? Very simple. We sold them the idea that Diners' was their club. If you are to enjoy it, we said, you must pay your bills immediately. This way you protect *your* club. We called upon Spanish pride. And it has worked. In fact, the most prompt payers of all are the Spanish members of the Diners' Club."

Many prophecies have been made as to what effect credit cards will have on the future. Perhaps the most disturbing and most plausible is the vision offered by Diners' president Bloomingdale. "Twenty years from now," he forecast, "there will be only two classes of people: those with credit cards and those who can't get them. Then there's going to be one hell of a split in society."

Even today one may ponder what Frank MacNamara's misplaced wallet hath wrought.

3 Big Brothers' Big Brother

A man's credit record follows him like his shadow.

From a pamphlet selling the services of the
Credit Bureau of Orlando, Florida

The extent to which some debt merchants are prepared to offer the convenience of credit can be illustrated in this unbelievable but true story. A furniture store in a Southern city is now selling television sets on the installment plan to inmates of a nearby state prison. The prisoners are not permitted to sign contracts, so all sales are based on character.

In advancing credit to a group of convicts, the retailer was indulging in America's greatest act of faith, accepting the promise to pay for goods or services after they have been received. Just how vast this act of faith is can be measured by the fact that at any one time one hundred million Americans have some kind of consumer debt. How the credit world insures that the faith is kept is known only to a few. It is, in part, an amazing tale of how a private group of citizens built up a file of dossiers that contain the financial and personal histories of nearly every American over twenty-one. It is the story of the credit bureaus which collect and sell to the nation's debt merchants the information they need to decide whether they will risk allowing you to buy something on time.

The enormous scope of this operation can be gleaned from the following. The Associated Credit Bureaus of America, the largest trade association of its kind, had a membership in the summer of 1960 that included 1,950 credit bureaus, 444 divisions which specialized in medical and dental credit and 1,270 collection bureaus. The credit bureaus alone employ an army of seventeen thousand who furnish nearly sixty-seven million oral and written credit reports a year. These operations are so vast that the combined floor space used by the Association's members covers fifty-four acres, or more than half the floor space contained in Chicago's huge Merchandise Mart, one of the largest buildings in the world.

Here perhaps is the most amazing part of all. The Association's combined membership covers every square inch of land in all fifty states. Thus, there is no place where you may live where a credit bureau could not unearth your past and present and rate your future. In addition, the Association has affiliated offices in Australia, Canada and Great Britain. The London office supplies Association members with information from all over Europe and covers a larger single area than any other member bureau in the world. Most important of all, the credit records of the Association's members number seventy million. Since many records contain the personal and financial background of both husband and wife, the number of histories in the credit bureau's files of the United States total one hundred and ten million, possibly more information on more people than has been collected by the Federal Bureau of Investigation and the Central Intelligence Agency combined. According to the Association, the Washington and regional offices of the F.B.I. are among the largest users of credit bureau services. If your name is not in the records of at least one credit bureau, it doesn't mean that you don't rate. What it does mean is that you are either under twenty-one or dead.*

Much of the success of our on-the-cuff economy hinges on how well the credit bureaus do their job. If the files of the nation's credit bureaus were destroyed tomorrow, it is conceivable that our entire economy would spin into a depression the likes of which would make the nineteen thirties appear as a polite economic burp. How important credit bureaus are can be shown by describing the way one works, the secrets it keeps, the methods it uses to collect and dispense information, and how this information is used to rate you.

The storehouse of New York City's financial respectability is located in a somewhat dingy looking office building in lower Manhattan. The Credit Bureau of Greater New York, a businessmen's co-operative, borders Union Square, once the home of the soap-box orator and the May Day rally. Though a mile and a half below Times Square, the mid-point of Manhattan Island, the Bureau, for its own purposes, is ideally located. North of the Bureau lies the bulk of the city's department stores which stretch along Thirty-fourth Street and then up Fifth Avenue. To the south are the courts of lower Manhattan and the merchant kings of downtown Brooklyn. Ordinarily, the geographical location would not

---

* In the winter of 1960 Britons were unnerved by a plan to institute a nationwide credit rating service, similar to those operating in the United States. Critics contended that such a service would invade the Englishman's cherished privacy. As one editorial writer noted, since Victorian times the average Briton has come to regard his financial standing as something secret and personal, an affair between himself and his banker and no one else. The journalist added, "The idea that, as in America, he should have some sort of public 'credit rating' is one that he (the Briton) properly resents."

seem important. However, one of the Bureau's services is to dispatch credit information with frequency and speed. Three times daily messengers make the rounds of the large stores delivering customers' credit histories and collecting the stores' inquiries.

A measure of how widespread on-the-cuff living has become can be seen in a glance at a partial list of the Bureau's twelve hundred members. To mention a few: Parke-Bernet Galleries (an art gallery), Cadillac Motors, Helena Rubinstein, Doubleday Book Stores, the New York Athletic Club, United Whelan Corporation, Edwin Jackson, Inc. (which sells fireplaces), Max Schling Inc. (florists), the A. & P., the Waldorf Astoria (one of twenty-six hotels), New York Life Insurance Company, Dominick & Dominick (brokers), Mme. Lilly Daché (women's hats); also opticians, shoe stores, restaurants, business schools, tobacconists, some thirty-nine women's wear stores, toy stores, theater ticket agencies, an advertising firm, and doctors and dentists. The only professional or business group not allowed to use the Bureau's credit files are lawyers. The Bureau fears that it might become involved with law suits by unhappy individuals who find that lawyers have used the information as part of litigation.

The history of the Credit Bureau of Greater New York, like the burgeoning of consumer credit itself, is comparatively recent. The Bureau in New York began operations in 1921 when a small group of merchants joined together to exchange information. (The first known credit bureau was started in London in 1803 by some enterprising tailors. Fifty-seven years later the first credit bureau in this country opened its doors in Brooklyn.)

The Credit Bureau of Greater New York is now the largest in the world, and certainly one of the most efficient. The

Bureau's amazing omniscience can be summed up with a few statistics. The territory the Bureau covers encompasses a fifty mile radius around the heaviest populated and busiest city in the country. Each year its staff handles over two million requests for credit information. Its files, which have been insured for one million dollars, contain dossiers on the spending and paying habits of seven million people, including two million visitors, from Bangkok, Thailand, to Bangor, Maine, who had occasion to come to New York to shop. In addition, the Bureau's Daily Litigation Bulletin Division, a separate court record department, keeps reports on fourteen million suits, judgments, bankruptcies, wage assignments and Federal tax liens. These records, compiled daily, are culled from the courts of Greater New York including Northern New Jersey. The Bureau also publishes each day, except weekends and holidays, *The Daily Litigation Bulletin,* a sad little newspaper that lists row upon row of commercial law suits. Its subscribers include finance companies, banking, lending and retail organizations and lawyers. (This is the only place attorneys are permitted to sign up for information.)

The man who oversees this never ending collection of dossiers, dates and debts is a debonair gentleman by the name of Rudolph Severa. It was during the budding of his career that he set his heart to brushing away the nettles and cobwebs that once littered the world of consumer credit. Rudolph Severa recalled his first experience when he tried to buy on time but couldn't. It was in the early nineteen twenties. He was eighteen and employed as a secretary and assistant accountant at *The Players,* a club for actors. As Severa recalls: "I needed a new suit and topcoat. So I went to a clothing store and offered to put one-third down and pay the balance over ten weeks. The manager said I couldn't do it because I was a minor. I had to get my father's signature. I told him I was earning more than my father. He only shook his head. Then I told him to call my employer. But he still wouldn't give me credit. I told him right then and there that if I ever became a credit manager I would institute a more elastic policy based on character and earning power."

Rudolph Severa's first major contribution to the onward sweep of on-the-cuff living came when he joined Macy's in 1939. Up to that time Macy's sold strictly for cash. Indeed, much of its fame rested on the promise to sell all of its merchandise for 6 per cent less for cash. Under a policy switch pushed by the late Beardsley Ruml, then treasurer of Macy's, the huge department store instituted what is called a time-cash payment plan which allowed customers to take eight to thirty-six months to pay. Severa was put in charge of the plan. It succeeded beyond expectations. Ten years later he was asked to assume the managership of the Credit Bureau of Greater New York.

"The purpose of a credit bureau," said Severa, "is to maintain a healthy consumer credit society. What we do is catalogue people according to their credit status. In a way we are like the F.B.I. which keeps a record of people who commit crimes. Here we are concerned with people who are poor risks and who might commit crimes against business."

It was when I visited the Bureau's file room that I first understood the passion of Rudolph Severa's life. The huge room was filled with bank upon bank of steel files. For Smith alone there are over fifteen drawers containing sixty thousand names. And unknown to the person who buys on time each card in short note form often bears the imprint of his or her life. It is all there: name, age, residence, marriage, divorce, inheritance, earnings, criminal record, bank account, date debts assumed and paid, slow pay, fast pay, no pay.* It was truly an investigator's paradise. The Bureau has even set aside a table for F.B.I. agents, Treasury men and the New York Police Department. They come there daily to copy information their agencies do not have.

The efficiency of the Bureau's operation when added to the totality and completeness of its files result in credit checks made at incredible speeds. Typical is this vignette in the sales life of A. Sulka & Co., a Park Avenue haberdasher. The customer, a stranger to the store, was unshaven, unkept and wore a baggy suit. He quickly picked out a scotch wool-flannel robe ($97.50) and two ties ($12.50 each). The salesman, who had been told to "charge it," politely excused himself, rushed to the store's credit manager and presented him with the sales slip. The credit manager, in turn, phoned the Credit Bureau, the line going direct to a rush-phone girl and the bank of files that contained the customer's name. Less than two minutes later, the salesman returned, smiling. Yes, indeed, Sulka would be most happy to charge it, for the credit manager had been told the customer had a four-figure bank account, a five-figure income and always paid his bills promptly.

When I visited the Credit Bureau there were twenty-six rush-phone girls working in the file room. Like circling bees extracting and feeding pollen, they would dip into the files, pluck out the appropriate card, and then read the information over a nearby phone. The pollen they gathered actually consisted of the private and personal histories of people who

* The Bureau adheres to a fairly strict weeding schedule. News items concerning weddings, inheritances and divorces are kept ten years. A derogatory report involving a single purchase under $25 is preserved for five years, over $25 for ten years. The only way the dead-beat debtor can restore his credit rating is to pay his debts.

planned to charge such items as a pair of shoes, a washing machine or a wedding dress.

Though life for the girls in the file room is routine, light moments do occur, like the man who offered as his credit references Brentano's, Brooks Brothers and a famous madam. His credit habits were excellent. Or the Georgia merchant who wanted to know whether a small dry-goods store called Gimbels in New York was good for $500. Then there was the credit manager who asked the Bureau to verify a customer's application to charge some merchandise. The Bureau solemnly told the manager that Harry S. Truman did live in the White House and that he was President of the United States.

All credit bureaus give out information only to members or government representatives. On occasion they will also do a personal favor for their own clients. Once a wealthy young widow inquired about the background of a gentleman who asked her if she would like to spend the week end with him. The Bureau fired back this succinct reply: "Age thirty-six, married, three small children, dependent." The widow spent the week end alone.

Another member, the owner of a successful dress shop, put in a request for a report on her husband. She assured the Bureau it had nothing to do with a secret romance. In fact, she and her husband were very much in love. It was just that her husband had asked her to invest some of her money in a new enterprise. The Bureau made a quick check and advised the woman her husband already had failed twice in the same business. The woman, of course, didn't invest.

The information the New York Bureau developed on the husband is what is called a "derogatory report." Over one million such items are added to the files each year. They range from defaulted debts and unpaid rent to bankruptcy and fraud. Much of the information concerning slow or delinquent paying habits is supplied by the Bureau members themselves. As part of their membership requirements they feed this information into the Bureau which in turn adds it to the files. There is a time when Macy's tells Gimbels and vice versa.

The members also are guarded by the Bureau's flash system which is used mainly to protect them against the loadup who speeds from store to store selecting merchandise and hoping that the saleman will not make an immediate credit check. One loadup, traveling up Fifth Avenue, got as far as Saks Fifth Avenue when the Bureau's flash notice stopped her. Several stores she had already visited had asked for a credit check. When the files showed the was a poor risk and her purpose became obvious, flash notices were sent to all stores along her route.

The flash notice, however, is rarely used. Most of the eight to ten thousand daily inquiries are answered by phone, messenger or through the mails. The Bureau also offers around-the-clock teletype service for members with a particularly heavy load of credit inquiries. This service generally is staggered, receiving requests for information one hour, answering them the next. Most of the members who use the teletype are banks which have large small-loan departments such as the First National City Bank, Manufacturers Trust, Industrial Bank of Commerce. Others include B. Altman's, a department store, and Mechanics Finance Company of Jersey City, a small-loan company. Since First National City's loan department works twenty-four hours a day, they send most of their inquiries over the teletype during the night. When the Bureau's girls start work in the morning, they can make an immediate check on the potential borrower's credit history.

Besides the huge volume of daily inquiries concerning the city's residents, the Bureau also handles a steady flow of credit checks for clients of bureaus in other cities. In addition, it forwards inquiries for its own customers who seek credit information on out-of-towners who visit New York. According to the statisticians of the Associated Credit Bureaus of America, the member bureaus annually handle over four million inter-bureau reports, not surprising when you consider that currently more than ten million Americans move out of their respective counties each year. As the industry is quick to note, no debtor can escape his credit history.

Next to the files, the most important department is the investigative section that checks out information not listed in the files. This section also works up credit histories of people who have not yet tried on-the-cuff living. The investigative department has thirty-eight inside sleuths plus four outside men. The inside investigators do all their checking over the phone. The outside investigators go where the phones do not. The inside and outside investigators handle nearly 250,-000 cases a year.

The head of the investigative staff is Howard Menzer, who gave up music for credit checking during the Depression. Menzer has never forgotten his first assignment, to investigate a young lady who said she was secretary to a music teacher. Music teachers generally are considered poor credit risks because their incomes are uncertain and hard to trace. Anyone who claims she is secretary to a music teacher is doubly suspect.

"It was raining that day," Menzer recalls, "and I had an umbrella and a raincoat. The apartment was on Madison Avenue and pretty swank. When I get there a maid comes out, takes my hat, coat, umbrella, and tells me to wait. While

I'm waiting a girl comes out. She wasn't wearing much more than she was born in. She takes one look at me and disappears. A minute later this elderly lady appears. She was just as cool as could be. This was supposed to be the music teacher. 'Oh, yes,' she said, 'the girl in question has been my secretary and companion for the last two years. A real hard worker.' I must have been pretty naïve because I went to the super to ask him what was going on. 'Don't know what the woman does,' he said. 'But an awful lot of young men go to her apartment for some kind of lessons.' "

Today Howard Menzer sits behind a desk, older and much wiser. The techniques he has learned over the years—and they are simple, but effective in gathering information—he passes on to younger and less experienced investigators. Most of the information the Bureau seeks can be obtained over the phone. The tools Menzer's staff uses are a small shelf of books. They serve as the keys to unlocking untold thousands of closet doors. One of the most effective is an unusual phone book. This directory first lists the street, then the names of the people who live on it and finally the phone numbers. With it an investigator locates the home address the credit applicant has listed and can check his neighbors' opinions of the applicant's character and habits. Usually there is little a neighbor doesn't know about the couple next door.

To learn whether an applicant pays his rent on time, an investigator switches to a real estate directory—each of New York's five boroughs has one—which lists the landlords of each building in the city. By calling the landlord, the investigator also will learn how long the applicant has lived at the address he's listed, as well as the number of dependents. If the applicant is a physician, dentist or lawyer, there are national directories which list the date a professional man was licensed to practice, his educational background and his office address. If the applicant is a commissioned officer in the Armed Forces, another directory will show where he entered the service, his birth date, temporary grade, the sum he is paid and the day when he receives his pay. Other mines of information include a *Dun and Bradstreet Directory* and the *Greater New York Industrial Directory,* which offers, among other nuggets, the number of people a firm employs, the area size it occupies and the names of its officers. If applicant lists his bank, the investigator can learn whether he keeps a regular checking acount and the average balance. A commercial bank will also tell an investigator the name of the company a credit applicant works for. Commercial banks, incidentally, are much freer in giving out information than savings banks. The only information a credit investigator generally is unable to obtain is the amount of money kept in a savings account unless, of course, it is volunteered by the credit applicant.

The yardstick all credit men apply to find out whether you are a good risk is summed up by the industry's three C's—Capital, Capacity and Character. According to Howard Menzer, Capital poses the question: Does a credit applicant have sufficient means to support himself or his family? Capacity asks the question: What is a man's ability to earn capital? A physician who has just begun to practice may be short on Capital but his Capacity or ability to earn may be excellent. The third question concerns an individual's Credit Character. Does he always pay his bills promptly? Has he ever been sued for non-payment of debt? A negative Credit Character can be more damaging than any other failing.

For the credit grantor the credit applicant most readily

welcomed is the person who shows a continuous history of debt and who has kept up with his payments. The credit manager does not think that the man who pays cash does so because he is thrifty and wants to stay out of debt. In the America of the nineteen-sixties the immediate proof of a man's probity and character is not judged by how much he saves but the frequency of his debts and whether he meets his monthly time payments.

Besides showing a history of debt the person who desires to live on time would do well to maintain certain economic standards as well as a behavior pattern defined by the debt merchants themselves. The following list of the more common danger signals to be used by credit managers in granting credit was compiled by the New York Bureau. If you or your friends have had difficulty buying on time, a review of this list may tell you why.

PERSONAL AND OCCUPATIONAL DANGER SIGNALS

1. Residence in: rooming house, hotel, in care of a friend, furnished apartment; slovenly home or section; place where questionable people are known to reside.
2. People in modest financial circumstances, with large dependent family.
3. Single persons living away from home on whom background information is not available.
4. Women who live under desirable conditions, who refuse or have failed to furnish sources of income or reliable references.
5. Divorced or separated women or widows who cannot supply financial references.
6. Individuals who try to impress the credit grantor with their extreme desirability as credit risks.

7. People who claim good incomes which cannot be verified, who do not carry a regular checking account.
8. Employment with a small unknown firm, or with a relative.
9. Generally unstable, hazardous, or transient occupations, such as bartender, dishwasher, taxi driver, longshoreman, day laborer, counterman, laundry worker, nurse, maid, waiter, housekeeper, garage worker.
10. Individuals who work in glamorous but relatively poor paying jobs, such as chorus girls or boys, models, dance hall hostesses.
11. People who make a living on fees earned at home, such as music teachers, tutors, masseurs, fortune tellers.
12. Salesmen who work on a commission basis only.

The Bureau notes that the danger signals "must be used intelligently and with good judgment; they suggest caution or careful investigation but are not all definite reasons for refusing credit." Nevertheless, the criteria used by credit men indicates the goals you should strive for: stolidity, stability and conformity. One can easily imagine the reception a credit manager would give to a freewheeling adventurer like Daniel Boone who while opening the West stopped off in St. Louis to buy provisions with a revolving credit account.

How important a part job stability and earning capacity play in granting credit can be seen from one more survey, given to me by a credit man. The survey was conducted by the Marketing Department of the University of Illinois in co-operation with the Associated Credit Bureaus of America. The following occupational brackets are listed according to the best credit risks, ranked in descending order. Here again are some of the criteria a credit man uses to rate your application. Parts of this list may surprise you.

OCCUPATION	AVERAGE ON A PERCENTAGE BASIS
In the 90 per cent range	
Business Executives	90.9
Accountants and Auditors	90.1
In the 80 per cent range	
Retail Managers (independent)	89.9
Chain Store Managers	89.9
Physicians, Dentists and Surgeons	89.3
Engineers, Chemical, Civil, etc.	89.2
General Farmers (owners)	88.7
Army and Navy Officers	87.7
Office Workers (clerks and stenographers)	87.1
College Professors and Instructors	87.0
Railroad Clerks	86.8
Skilled Factory Workers	86.8
Post Office Employees	85.4
Railroad Workers (trainmen)	84.7
Hotel and Restaurant Managers	84.4
Other Schoolteachers	83.7
Clergymen	82.5
Nurses	82.5
Public Officials (Federal, State, Local)	82.1
Retail Salespeople	81.5
Printers	80.1
In the 70 per cent range	
Lawyers and Judges	78.3
Traveling Salesmen	77.0
Plumbers	76.9
Policemen and Firemen	76.4
Carpenters	74.8
Guards and Watchmen	74.3

General Farmers (tenants)	73.1
Truck and Bus Drivers	71.6
Soldiers and Sailors (enlisted men)	71.0
Unskilled Factory Workers	70.7
Janitors	70.5
Section Hands	70.1

In the 60 per cent range

Plasterers	69.7
Barbers	68.1
Coal Miners	67.7
Common Laborers	67.5
Bartenders	63.8
Musicians	63.2
Domestic Servants	63.1
Painters	61.8
Farm Laborers	60.3

The comparatively poor ratings shown by high school and elementary school teachers (83.7 per cent) and clergymen (82.5 per cent), doesn't mean that they are less honest than business executives (90.9 per cent), but that on the average they are paid less for their services. Hence, the lower esteem in which they are held in the eyes of the credit grantor.

A different explanation, though, is offered for the relatively poor credit rating shown by lawyers and judges (78.3 per cent) which may be compared, for example, to the medical profession (89.3 per cent). As one credit man put it: "Lawyers and judges know so damned much. They know their legal rights and obligations. For example, under the law a married man is generally responsible for supplying the necessities of life to his mate. Let's say a woman buys a fur coat on time. If she is a socialite, the fur coat will be declared a necessity of life and her husband will be held responsible. If she doesn't travel in society, he may not be responsible for the debt. Another difficulty is that lawyers often live on the few fat fees they are expecting but haven't received."

The only class of people that the Bureau gives special attention is the neon and klieg light profession—actors, directors, producers, playwrights and models. The expert who runs the Bureau's theatrical department is Selma Jacobs, a credit investigator of extraordinary calm, patience and good sense. Her first real involvement with the arts came when, graduating from Hunter College, she went to work for an elderly actor who had opened a theatrical credit office. Within a year Miss Jacobs joined the Bureau where she has since developed her unique specialization. Today, more than twenty years later, Selma Jacobs' personal knowledge of the fiduciary state of Hollywood and Broadway probably surpasses the combined intelligence of the entire Internal Revenue Service.

As I sat near her desk, surrounded by the catalogues and directories of stardom, Miss Jacobs explained the purpose of her special calling. "Theatrical people," she said, "are different. Often they do not get a weekly salary and they move about a great deal. Both are usually considered danger signals among creditors. Now, to know their credit standings I have to know where to go for information. If someone claims he's an actor and I don't know him, I'll check Actor's Equity or AFTRA. Or I'll call the theatrical agent and if necessary hold an interview. You see I read all the theatrical trade papers, know all the producers' offices. They trust me with the information. An actor walks into Lord and Taylor's or Saks Fifth Avenue and he's buying. A credit manager must make a quick decision. He calls me and within a few minutes I tell him what kind of a risk the actor is."

Miss Jacobs insists it is wrong to think that all actors are bad risks. As a whole, she says, they are not worse than any other group in any other field. In fact in some ways they are better. They spend more. "There are people in the theater," Miss Jacobs offered, "who you can hold up as worthy examples to the credit world. Katherine Cornell, Lunt and Fontanne, to name a few."

One point everybody at the Bureau emphasized, that no matter who the credit customer may be, actor, physician, clergyman, lawyer or short-order cook, most people do pay their debts. According to Rudolph Severa the majority of credit reports that are fed into the Bureau's files are favorable. Losses in retail charge accounts, for example, average a minuscule one-fourth to three-eights of one per cent. It would appear that most of us are innately honest. But are we?

4 *The Specialists in Friendly Anxiety*

> You can repossess a car, but you can't repossess a baby.
>
> *A medical bill collector explaining his problems as quoted in* The Wall Street Journal.

"You can't get away from the use of fear in collecting bills. We can't offer the debtor anything positive like a nice frosty cake. We can only offer relief from anxiety, and, therefore, the collector has to make sure that a certain amount of anxiety is present."

So spoke Dr. E. H. Barnes, a former college psychology instructor. Dr. Barnes belongs to a small group of psychologists who have anointed the credit industry with their special talents. The new look in consumer credit, they have become the purveyors of the latest psychological techniques used to make debtors pay up.

As research director of National Accounts System, Inc., which controls seven collection agencies in the Chicago area, Dr. Barnes has been eminently successful. When he first started to work for National Accounts, the organization collected $50,000 a month in overdue bills. Two years later, the figure had risen to $170,000 per month. According to

Gordon Fletcher who heads National Accounts: "To the best of my knowledge our recovery rate is the highest in the nation. We are averaging 79 per cent collection on those accounts we can locate. The type of people we have employed and our collection methods have given us the prestige to gain accounts of people who have never hired a collection agency. Creditors think that with our modern methods and professional personnel we can collect bills without offending the customer." One of the groups which has approved the organization's and Dr. Barnes' new methods is the Chicago Dental Society.

Speaking before a conference held by the National Retail Merchants Association, the psychologist noted that just because most people pay their bills doesn't mean that honesty is a general trait. Honest behavior, he observed, is specific to a situation. A man may be punctilious about paying his debts, but embezzle the money to do it from his employer. "Actually," said Dr. Barnes, "prompt payment of debts among the majority of people is the result of a complex process of social conditioning involving parental teaching, social pressures, vague fears of legal consequences and so on. The fact that such a large proportion of the people do pay their bills and pay them reasonably promptly attests to the success of this social conditioning. In a way it is remarkable that so many people have learned so well and behave so predictably."

Just how well the consumer has been conditioned to fulfill his credit obligations can be attested to by the fact that during the Depression non-payment of consumer debts rarely rose above 5 per cent. Indeed, if the consumer did not generally pay what he owed, the entire elaborate structure of what is now fifty-six billion dollars in consumer credit could never have been built. Further, if the consumer credit explosion is to continue, the debt merchants must insure that anxiety over unpaid bills remains a permanent fixture in the American psyche.

Arousing anxiety in the delinquent debtor is a tricky business. On the one hand the bill collector must make the customer pay up. At the same time, he doesn't want to antagonize him, so that he will incur his future debts elsewhere. As Dr. Timothy Costello, professor of psychology at New York University, described it: "The collection agency's approach must involve a sense of friendly urgency. He must keep a positive pleasant feeling and also arouse anxiety."

The friendly part of the approach, according to Dr. Costello, is to reserve "a little time for listening. Frequently people want to get something off their chest." Also the bill collector should avoid arguing with the debtor and should assume from the outset the most, not the least, from a delinquent customer.

To instill anxiety and yet remain on friendly terms with the debtor calls for several approaches. Basic to each approach is the use of certain evocative words or phrases. Dr. Barnes, for example, has been experimenting with word association tests. "When I want to be nice," he says, "I call it a small account. When I want to humiliate, I call it a petty account."

The initial approach used by every collection department or agency is to play upon the prestige and importance of being able to obtain credit. The threat that this privilege may be denied in the future can be a blow against one's self-esteem—"they don't trust me"—and a slur against one's earning power. But even more important, it includes a play upon the debtor's fear that he might be denied credit in case of an emergency. The following letter offered by the National Retail Credit Association for use by the credit departments at hospitals manages to say all of the above and still appear the Samaritan:

> Dear Mr. Patient:
> A good credit standing is a priceless asset. It is a wonderful feeling to know that when credit is needed, credit will be gladly given.
> Of course, to keep one's credit bright and shining, it is necessary to pay bills exactly as agreed.
> And that includes hospital bills, too! For one reason or another, your account with this hospital has not been paid. You know those reasons, but—we don't.
> We would be glad to have you tell us . . . and to work out a mutually satisfactory arrangement with you.
> Don't allow delay to dull your fine credit record.
>
> Cordially yours,
(Signature)
Name typed
Title

For some recalcitrant debtors, their anxiety threshold may have to be reached by other means, such as a phone call or a visit by a collector. Since almost all debt merchants have their own collection department, it is only as a last resort that the creditor will turn over an account to a professional collection agency. The process continues—more mailed notices, each taking a harsher tone, more phone calls, perhaps another visit. If the debtor still refuses to pay, the wraps are removed and he is told simply and directly that if he doesn't meet his obligations he will be taken to court. This is the creditor's most effective weapon. If it's merchandise the debtor purchased, the creditor may be able to repossess the goods. Finally, the creditor may garnishee the debtor's wages.

As a means of instilling anxiety and fear, the garnishment has few parallels in our society. Under a garnishee, a creditor with court approval may call upon an employer to deduct a part of a debtor's wages which is then turned over to the creditor. Though the law varies from state to state,* a number permit garnishments which leave the debtor a bare subsistence wage.

The garnishee is used with such abandon that one company in Chicago, Inland Steel, has set up a separate department just to handle the problem. The plant employs 22,000. During 1960 an estimated 3,000 garnishments were brought against Inland's workers. Under the 1959 Illinois law a garnishment action "catches" any earnings the company owes an employee at the time of service and during the next seven days. Everything the employee earns during those seven days must be turned over to the creditor except $45. Tax deductions also are exempted. If the debt is not paid with the first garnishment, another and still another is filed until the debt is paid.

Before Inland set up its program to help its employees, many of the plant's workers found themselves in endless debt. One debt merchant received $7 from each garnishment he slapped on a particular worker. But each time a judgment was obtained, the creditor added $6 for court costs. Thus the employee's debt was only reduced $1. Since he owed $187, he faced 187 garnishments before he would have been free. Another employee owed $160.32. Each time his wages were garnished, the creditor received $5. However, the creditor added a $6 court cost. Thus, each garnishment put the em-

---

* Garnishments are illegal in only four states: Connecticut, Florida, Pennsylvania and Texas.

ployee $1 deeper into debt. By the time his full debt of $160 was garnisheed, instead of being solvent he would actually owe twice the amount, or $320.

Many companies, though, are not as understanding as Inland Steel. *The Credit Union Bridge,* the official publication of the Credit Union National Association, made a survey of garnishments in four cities—Birmingham, Washington, D.C., San Francisco and Indianapolis. The magazine found that during 1957 there were more than eighty-five thousand garnishment cases. In the District of Columbia an average of one thousand garnishments were filed each week. One Birmingham business leader reported that a garnishment was filed to collect a ten-cent debt.

What happens to a man whose wage is garnisheed? Many employers, said the magazine, look upon garnishment as a cause for immediate dismissal. In some instances an employer will permit three garnishments prior to discharge. Others are less lenient and dismiss after the first judgment. Many firms simply object to the extra cost involved in the additional bookkeeping. John Kearney, chairman of the Committee for Fair Credit Practices in Illinois, recalled this conversation with an employer while testifying before the recent U.S. Senate hearing on consumer credit.

> Virtually daily, I speak to people in extreme hardship cases. Virtually daily, I also speak to employers, many of whom, such as Inland Steel, honestly try to do everything that they can for the employee.
>
> However, I would like to cite one case. I will not mention this employer's name by any means. I was talking to him on the telephone just last week. I asked him, "Do you have any credit difficulties in your concern?"
>
> He said, "No, I never have any difficulties, assignments with

garnishments, with anything like that, because I have a system. As quick as I get a paper, I call the person in and fire him."

I said to him, "Is this not rather hard, to lose people that you have had for many years?"

"I had a woman," he told me, "who was working for me for twenty-five years, a very valuable employee. She cosigned for her son. I have taught her a very valuable lesson when I discharged her and showed her what her son really was."

This particular woman lost her job, twenty-five years seniority, and besides that, the employer was himself becoming an agent in undermining the family morale and family solidarity.

Garnishment of a worker's wages may not only mean impoverishment for himself but his family as well. Wythe F. Cooper, the assistant director of the Madison Street office of the Cook County Department of Welfare, knows the meaning of this credit grantor's weapon. He estimates that a high percentage of the desertion cases coming to the attention of his office in applications for aid to dependent children are not true desertions. Rather they are "desertion because of debt" cases, where the father of the family discovers he can no longer provide for his family with the small amount that is left from his garnished pay check. He leaves his family so they can receive welfare payments while he ekes out his existence in some other part of the city. As John Kearney observed: "The human suffering that is caused, the breakup of families, the breakdown of individual morale, the deprivation of the very necessities of life, are all traceable, in many instances, to so-called easy payment plans which wind up being very difficult indeed."

Perhaps most disturbing of all is the similarity between the punishment afflicted on today's debtor and the man who could not pay his debts just a little over a century ago. The last debtor's prison in the United States was abolished by the Commonwealth of Massachusetts in 1855. It was not uncommon for a delinquent debtor to be put in a cell without bedding or fuel, where his companions were a parade of disease-infested rats, and a day's meal was limited to a bowl of soup.

Today, except in Maine, no man can be imprisoned because he didn't meet his debts. But how does he fare? In 1829, when almost no state was complete without its debtors' jail, some 75,000 people out of a population of twelve million were arrested in the United States for nonpayment of their debts. During 1959, exactly 130 years later, in the city of Chicago with a population of about four million, some 58,000 garnishment suits were filed. This, incidentally, is more than double the number of garnishments registered in the nation's then second largest city in 1950. In 1829, approximately 13,000 delinquent debtors in the United States were sentenced to jail. It is fair to assume that in America of 1960 many times that number were improverished because of the garnishee. Today's debtor may not only find his livelihood taken away from him but his family may be forced to subsist on the public dole. For the "friendly" debt collector there always remains the ultimate weapon, economic destitution.

5 *Finders, Keepers*

> For months we had been trying to repossess this
> farmer's car. Every time we asked where he had hid
> it, he'd just tell us he couldn't find no trace of it
> nowhere. But we kept after him. Finally, he led us
> to a field where he began digging. You know what
> he had done? He had buried the damn thing in a
> hole, covered it with canvas, then filled the hole
> with dirt. It's amazing what some people will do.
>
> *An auto repossession man recounting his
> experiences.*

One day an employee at a Canadian collection agency was
reading the death notices in her local newspaper. She stopped
abruptly at the family name of one of the deceased. The
name was the same as that of a young man who had bought a
$75 diamond ring from a jeweler on time and then disap-
peared. An agency representative was ordered to attend
the funeral services. As it turned out, the man who died was
the father of the young debtor. The man from the collection
agency followed the young man from the funeral parlor to
the cemetery where his father was buried and then back to
his home where he finally presented him with a bill. It was
paid in full on the spot.

For the skip tracer—the man or woman who hunts disappearing debtors or merchandise—the adventures of the auto
repossession man and the Canadian collection agency are not
unusual. The pro of pros within the hierarchy of bill collecting, the skip tracer must first locate and identify his prey be-

fore the specialists in friendly anxiety can begin their labor. Frequently the skip tracer will be employed by a collection agency and will shift to the role of the bill collector once the debtor has been found. His primary job, though, is to seek out the missing debtor or goods. Like the bounty hunter, the skip tracer may spend years in a roving search that could take him to cities and hamlets across the land. As in the tale of the cat and the mouse, his tools are stealth, subterfuge and bait to nibble on.

There are just a few places where a skip tracer will not venture. One stopped only when he discovered the man he was hunting had moved to Tbilisi, Georgia, USSR. Another skip tracer quit after he found that the debtor had fled to Greece, taking with him the car he still owed payments on.

Such cases are rare, though, since most skips do not travel that far. If they remain within the confines of the United States, they almost invariably are caught. Frequently, when the missing debtor is found he not only acknowledges his identity but returns the money he owes. One skip was on a luxury liner sailing for Europe. The boat was 500 miles off shore when he was paged to the ship-to-shore phone. The man on the other end was a skip tracer. The debtor was so shocked by the call that he admitted who he was and agreed to pay up. The skip tracer, like the Royal Mounted Police, almost always gets his man.

The persistence with which skip tracers work can be seen in The Case of the Overdue Furniture Account as related by A. M. Tannrath, author of the skip tracer's classic, "How to Locate Skips and Collect." The account was sixteen years overdue. What's more, the statute of limitations on the debt had long since run out and the collection could not be legally enforced. While examining the skip tracer's ledger sheet, which hadn't been worked for thirteen years, Tann-rath noticed an almost undecipherable scrawl. Applying a reading glass, he was able to make out an address in a small town in Minnesota. A registered letter followed. A few days later Tannrath received the registry return card. The skip had been located. The account was closed when the skip paid $150 of the $188 that was due.

A distinction must be made between the skip or debtor who vanishes by design and the person who disappears by accident. Many debtors whom the skip tracer seeks do not intend to renege on their obligations. As so often happens, they simply forget to leave a forwarding address. Once found and approached they readily pay up. The major problem for the skip tracer is that small coterie of debtors who are both skips and dead beats. The typical dead beat will cloak himself in anonymity by conspiring with his friends, neighbors and relatives to conceal his whereabouts. Frequently the dead beat will move to another address, and even another town. One dead beat had changed his residence but was located by a tracer who impersonated a priest. The skip tracer phoned the debtor's mother telling her that her son had just won a Cadillac in a parish raffle. The mother could hardly wait to give the tracer her boy's new address.

Though most skips are amateur crooks, several have turned into fulltime credit swindlers. A skip tracer told me that she knew of a case where a credit crook actually took college courses on consumer credit to learn ways of beating the system.

One of the cleverest schemes, reported recently by the National Better Business Bureau, concerned a swindler who hired a telephone answering service. He explained that he was not in the office most of the time and thus was unable to take calls, then added that many of the calls he did receive came from banks and merchants who were checking up on his employees seeking credit. He proceeded to give the answering service a fictitious list of employees and such information as their length of service and the salaries they earned. Next he made the rounds of the local merchants, ordering goods on credit in the names of his "employees." When the merchants called to verify the credit information, the answering service confirmed the employment details given on the credit applications. One swindler, using this scheme, managed to obtain nearly twenty thousand dollars in loans from banks in just one community.

To catch the dedicated skip and dead beat, the skip tracer willingly disguises his identity, sends ruses through the mail and even hires informers. One of the hardest skips to locate is the itinerant gypsy. Two large auto sales finance companies managed to solve this problem when their skip tracing departments hired gypsy informers. Though most gypsies are considered poor risks, some still can buy cars on time. The automobiles they prefer generally fall into the Cadillac-Lincoln class. The informers not only know who in their tribe is cheating the finance company but the phone numbers of the skip tracing departments. All the informer has to do is contact the company and, depending upon the year and make of the car, he receives from two hundred to five hundred dollars for turning in his fellow gypsy.

Besides gathering bits of information from gypsies, disgruntled relatives, friends, neighbors and business associates, the skip tracer may choose to pose in any number of guises, all of whch hide his true identity. *The Wall Street Journal* records these choice parts played by one skip tracer: a Western Union agent with an important message to deliver, an express clerk with a package, the manager of a supermarket and a bank executive. The skip tracer went on to describe the results he gets from his impersonations.

"Once," he recalls, "I was trying to locate the assets of a minister who was delinquent on a house-moving bill to the tune of several hundreds of dollars. A minister's income is awfully hard to put your fingers on so I thought I'd try to find out where he banked. Well, I called him and told him I was the manager of so-and-so bank and that there were not enough funds in his account to cover a check he had passed. He was irate. Said it wasn't possible because he didn't have an account at that bank. 'That's funny,' I said, 'the check is right here in front of me. You're so-and-so, aren't you?' I asked, and he replied, yes he was, and I asked him where, then, he did keep his account. He replied, without a suspicion in the world, but then he insisted on seeing the check. I told him to come on down and have a look at it. I can imagine the poor fellow's face when they told him in the bank they didn't have anyone by that name and knew nothing of any check of his that bounced. Anyway, we attached the account and collected."

The skip tracer will employ a variety of tricks and subterfuges to locate a missing debtor, to make the skip identify himself or to gather information about the skip's place of employment or holdings so that his wages or assets can be attached. To keep costs down, the dead beat sleuth does most of his tracing over the phone or through the mails. Here are just a few of the techniques employed by the skip tracer:

To make the skip identify himself, the skip tracer may pose as the representative of a moving company. The skip tracer will call to check the address for the delivery of household furniture. The dead beat is expected to blurt, "You've got the wrong party. This is Mrs. Green at Nineteen Bingo Boulevard."

To locate a delinquent debtor's employer, the skip tracer may impersonate a woman's voice. The "woman" may say something like "I'm calling for an employment agency. We understand Mr. Brown has just lost his job." Mr. Brown's wife will exclaim, "Lost his job? Why, Willy's been employed by The Happy Acre Cemeteries for the last fifteen years."

Another skip tracer mailed out a "gift certificate" to missing debtors, promising a supply of razor blades for the people participating in his study of the razor-blade market. The debtor was asked what brand he used and whether he was "influenced" by radio or TV advertising. Two other not so innocent questions were also asked: the recipient's address and the address of his employer.

Still another gimmick used to flush a quarry is to send only the second page of a letter written in longhand. It reads:

2.

Let me hear from you at once, as it is important.

Yours truly,
John Jones
Mokena, Illinois

A. M. Tannrath, who suggested the letter with the missing page, notes in his book for budding skip tracers: "We found this tracer to be very successful, because the recipient would become curious, thinking that the first page of the letter had been inadvertently left out. This letter should be sent to all of the addresses you have. It is advisable to have a mailing address and name other than your own, providing you are sending your mail from a large city. We used an address in a small town in Illinois and also a post office box in the city."

If the letter with the missing page doesn't work, Tannrath suggests this followup:

Dear Mr. Smith:
    Please answer my letter at once, as it is important.

Yours truly,
John Jones,
Mokena, Ill.

"If you have had no reply after ten days," Tannrath advises, "or if the letter has not been returned, then a certified letter is in order. When you are tracing and not collecting, your enclosure will be a blank piece of paper."

Perhaps the most successful gimmick of all is the bait letter that appears to offer something of value. One that was used with considerable success consisted of an envelope so thin it appeared transparent. The check inside was worth exactly ten cents. The letter would be sent via registered mail. Most debtors found it almost impossible not to sign for the letter. Or if it was received by relatives or friends, they couldn't resist forwarding it. One skip tracer, using a similar gimmick, managed to draw seven hundred replies weekly out of twenty-one hundred mailings. The Federal Trade Commission stepped in on the grounds that such tricks were misleading and not in the public interest. The Federal agency was upheld in court, the judge exclaiming: "It would be fantastic to suggest that one delinquent and previously unresponsive debtor out of three would reply if he thought he was furnishing information to his creditors for a net return of ten cents . . . The letter succeeds in conveying the false impression it must convey in order to achieve its purpose."

Certainly one of the most objectionable of all the skip tracer's techniques has been the use of phony forms and questionnaires with high-sounding but non-existent government titles, such as "Bureau of Records of Employment" or "National Service Bureau." Often these forms also carried an imprint similar to that of the American eagle. The forms would be meter-mailed from headquarters in Washington, D.C. One of the firms which used such methods was called before the Federal Trade Commission. The firm, arguing in its defense, said that the Washington telephone directory lists forty-eight firms with the words "United States" and fifty-five using the word "Federal." It also noted thirteen differences between the eagle on its mailing cards and the eagle on the Great Seal of the United States.

The F.T.C., though, was not impressed. The federal agency noted that there are at least four different eagles used by the Government on coinage alone. "We are compelled to conclude," the Commission declared, "that all these factors, including the fictitious names of nonexistent offices from which the forms purport to emanate, the use of the words United States as part of one such name, the phraseology of each form, the use of an eagle thereon, and the Washington, D.C. return address and mailing tend, in conjunction with one another, to foster the erroneous belief and perpetrate the deception that respondent's fictitious offices are part of the United States government."

The F.T.C.'s war with skip tracers has been raging now for nearly two decades. The Commission, of course, feels that the man who uses credit with intent to defraud should pay back the money he owes. At the same time it also insists that the skip's unethical behavior cannot excuse the skip tracer's use of subterfuge and lies. As the federal agency put it: "The laudable purpose of assisting merchants to recover financial losses by reason of defaulting debtors does not justify the perpetration of deceit on these debtors."

Despite the F.T.C.'s constant battle, skip tracers deceit continues to flourish. As soon as the questionable activities of several skip tracers are exposed, others take their place. The result is a giddy dance in which the federal government pursues the unethical skip tracer who in turn is running after the disappearing debtor. As long as on-the-cuff living plays such an important part in our lives, the macabre chase will continue as one more step in the national vertigo.

From what has been said so far it would appear that much of the effort expended by the skip tracer and the collection man is hardly worthwhile considering the monetary gain involved. This would seem particularly true when you examine the following figures compiled by the U. S. Department of Commerce. Without attaching a debtor's wages, a collection man will bring in two out of three debts on which no payments have been made for six months. He will collect less than half of all debts that have been delinquent for one year. By the end of two years he will collect less than one out of three debts; three years, less than one out of five; five years, one out of one hundred unpaid debts. This means that on the average only 67 cents of each dollar's worth of debt at the end of six months will be collected. At the end of one year the value of a dollar's debt drops to 45 cents, and by the end of five years it is worth only one cent.

The professional debt collector, though, views the figures more as a challenge than a deterrent. He may use them as a sales pitch in approaching merchants who try to do their own collection work. These figures also help explain his fairly high fees. Most debt collectors keep between 20 and 50 per cent of whatever they take in. On an account that's over one-and-a-half years old, they pocket half. Further, much time and manpower is saved through the use of the nation's credit bureau files. As noted in Chapter 3, over twelve hundred collection agencies in the country have at their disposal the credit histories of 110 million people.

According to the head of one of the larger collection bureaus in the country, his staff of twenty handles more than sixty thousand claims a year, one-third of which bring in a 50 per cent fee. Currently, his agency collects $350,000 annually. In addition, his skip tracer, a woman, locates between one hundred fifty and two hundred people monthly. "Because she's a woman," he said, "she can ask the damnedest questions and get away with them."

As suggested earlier most delinquent debtors and skips are likely to be people trapped in the charge-it web. They may be overloaded, having bought too much on time, or they may be faced with a financial emergency caused by illness or loss of job. The average delinquent debtor has neither the desire nor the ability to match wits with the professional bill collector, already armed with the skills and tricks of his trade. Collecting most delinquent debts is as easy as plucking apples off a tree.

Though the typical debtor is docile when dunned, he will naturally become incensed when the bill collector requests payment for something he claims he did not purchase. The following letter actually was received by one collection agency.

To whom it may concern,
I am getting very sick of receiving demanding letters from your company. I hope that this letter brings about a stop to this whole matter. I never placed an order for XYZ records, so I do not owe you $4.45. *You are ruining my reputation and good name.* I hope that I don't have to put this matter into the hands of my attorney.

The letter was written under the letterhead of an Eastern penitentiary by an inmate.

Of all the reasons why people overextend themselves in debt the most common is the heady temptation offered by the credit genie. The following outpouring of this benighted male came about when his wife received two collection letters from the same store on the same day. One letter was a form letter signed by William Dunn, the other by an actual collection man. His reply is a classic.

Dear Messrs:

It was with a sense of profound shock and dismay that I opened and read the communications which arrived simultaneously (a startling coincidence, no doubt) and which were addressed to the woman with whom I have shared both bed and board for lo these thirteen years. You will accept my profound apologies if it is I rather than she who answers these missives, for she is far too distraught to render an intelligible reply. You will, I trust, also pardon me for addressing you jointly, because the state of my unhappy finances is such that I dare not try this battered typewriter ribbon twice. Let me say, too, that it is with considerable pleasure that I find it possible to communicate with two living men rather than with an abstract and monstrous corporation.

These amenities having been observed, let me now proceed

to the business at hand. For far too many years than I care to calculate I (or to be more precise, my wife) has been a thrall to Bloomingdale's, and this relationship has been an incubus whose power has freighted my dreams with visions worthy of a Baudelaire, a Poe, a Verlaine. This thralldom has existed since the companion of my hearth found to her delighted incredulity that it was possible to purchase goods at your New Rochelle branch without paying real money. You will, of course, note the underlined word in the previous sentence and may not understand.

Mrs. B (I call her Alice and since you have always addressed her as Mrs. B, I wish, in the fading moments of a relationship which I shall ever hold dear, for you to know her given name), a tender and sweet but wholly naïve woman, has ever found it impossible to recognize that when one charges for items (or writes checks—but then that is an equally long and unhappy story), one must eventually pay for them. An innocent victim of what would appear to be an increasingly international conspiracy which rivals Communist skullduggery, the credit racket (no offense meant to you two who must, as I, earn your bread), she wandered monthly and blithely through Bloomingdale's plucking goods from the glittering counters much as a child plucks daisies and buttercups from a vernal hillside. Heedless and with a happy smile on her rosy lips, she frolicked through fields of shoes, stockings, perfumes, girdles, sweaters, blouses, glassware, greeting cards, snow suits, gloves, lipsticks, powders, and assorted unguents.

As husbands will, I honored the results of her pleasure journeys, which brought such smiles of sweet contentment to her cheeks. I must confess, however, that as the months passed I found it increasingly difficult to hide the pain which stabbed as a riven nail at the conclusion of each lunar orbit when it became necessary to mail to your employers the results of my travails in the workaday world.

Now, however, dear Messrs. . . . , the time has come for me to bid both you and Bloomingdale's a fond and fervent farewell. My darling wife and I have agreed (she, under some duress, you will not be displeased to learn) to return to certain virtues which seem to live in most moderns only as the faintest of memories. One of these virtues is that one spends the money one has and avoids the odious Debtor's Prison. This being the case, it is time to retire that red-encased charga-plate, just as Red Grange hung up old 77. We shall, be assured and if it be your will, give it a place of honor in our home. I can see it now gleaming fitfully on our wall as it catches fire from the dying embers of our fading television tube, another household god.

I am certain that you must feel that I have been intolerably long-winded, but, gentlemen, please do not heap scorn on an old and retiring player of the charga-game. Like old 77, I was good in my time.

Now, as for the $42.32 which I must unhappily own that I do indeed owe you (surely, Mr. Dunn, there was no *real* doubt in your mind on that score), I hereby do promise and swear (my hand on my defunct charga-plate) that on October 1, 1959 I shall remit said sum and thereby erase from your records my brand of shame. If this date does not meet with your approval, I shall surrender my television tube on account, although I suggest that step only with diffidence, for my two children have been known to pierce the buttocks of many a repair man.

And now, dear, dear, dear Bloomingdale's, good night and may choirs of angels sing you to your rest.

Your most obedient and humble servant,
L. B.

It is rare that the delinquent debtor has the power or means to strike back when the bill collectors become too insistent. On the few occasions that a debtor does seek his revenge, the results can be devastating. Such was the case of a man who bought a wildcat on time from a fashionable cat store that specialized in everything from Siamese to lions. When the customer refused to pay, the store turned the account over to a collection agency. The wildcat's new master wanted to return the animal. But the agency insisted its policy called for cash, not the merchandise. A decided mistake, for this piece of merchandise was capable of attacking and killing a horse. After a few more phone calls from the collection agency, the delinquent debtor drove to the store, tossed in the wildcat, quickly shut the door and fled. The four salesmen inside nearly climbed the walls before the animal fell into a cage. To add further injury, the collection agent dunned the store for his efforts to get the bobcat buyer to pay up.

In this case the debt collector was unharmed. Others, however, are not so fortunate. One outside collection man showed me a series of scars he had received while making his appointed rounds for a small-loan company in Newark. While interviewing one delinquent debtor in her kitchen, he was suddenly greeted by a huge police dog. He managed to escape only after the dog had opened five wounds. When he staggered to the street, the vessels in his arms and legs hemorrhaging, he pleaded for help. Passers-by who had seen him before and knew his calling, exclaimed: "You can die." He finally reached his car and drove to the city hospital, where he was treated by an intern. The intern had done such a hasty job that he hemorrhaged in the hospital phone booth while calling his office.

When the debt collector had finished his tale, I asked him why he was still in the business. He replied, "I love it. You meet all sorts of interesting people."

6 *The Wonderland of Credit*

> "A hill *ca'n't* be a valley, you know. That would be nonsense—"
> The Red Queen shook her head. "You may call it 'nonsense' if you like," she said, "but *I've* heard nonsense compared with which that would be as sensible as a dictionary!"
>
> *From* Through the Looking Glass
> *by Lewis Carroll*

Perhaps the most important single phenomenon concerning on-the-cuff living is this: When it comes to knowing the cost of credit, the American consumer is undoubtedly one of the most ignorant, illiterate and easily deceived. This is true despite the fact that we purchase more on credit than all the peoples of all other lands combined. What this means in dollars and cents can be stated simply. At the end of 1960 the total volume of consumer debt (both mortgage and consumer credit) was over $195 billion. A one-half per cent reduction in the interest rate would mean a savings of some one billion dollars. Yet we are unable to keep a fraction of that amount because almost all of us are totally incapable of shopping wisely for credit. The irony is that in his own country the American consumer who buys on time acts and is treated like an ignorant tourist in a foreign land. Incapable of even translating the value of the coin he uses, he readily accepts the first price given him.

The consumer's abysmal ignorance of the cost of credit has been pointed up in survey after survey. One study published in the *Journal of Marketing* in October, 1955, was made in the twin cities of Champaign and Urbana, Illinois. Of the 311 families who responded to the random sample, 136, almost half, had made use of credit in 1953 or were paying for credit contracted before that time. Jean Mann Due, the author of the survey, reports: "Although the respondents readily answered questions relating to amounts of credit contracted, approximately two thirds of the users of installment credit did not know the amount of the carrying charges or interest rate on their most recent installment purchase."

The Illinois study is backed up by a nationwide survey made six years later by The Survey Research Center of the University of Michigan. George Katona, the author of the Michigan survey, is a professor of economics and psychology. One question his staff posed in November, 1959, to consumers was: "Do you happen to know how much interest or carrying charges one has to pay to buy a car on time; suppose you need a thousand dollars which you would repay monthly over two years; about how much do you think the interest or carrying charges would be each year?"

Professor Katona went on to observe that 39 per cent did not give an answer from which a precise estimate of the cost of installment credit could be derived. Many of these people simply said they did not know, others gave such wide ranges in their answers that the replies could not be used. The survey notes that of the remaining 61 per cent of those interviewed approximately one out of five said that the cost of installment credit is 6 per cent per year or less, about the same number placed the cost between 7 and 12 per cent, one out of six thought it was 13 per cent or higher. Said Professor Katona: "Obviously many people believed that the cost of installment buying is lower than it actually is." Are these well founded opinions? he asks and observes:

"On practically any item of knowledge or information we have studied, we find that high-income people, people with college education, and people with personal experience in the matter studied are better informed than other people. But this finding is not sustained on the item of cost of installment credit. We find that 31 per cent of people with more than $10,000 income, likewise 31 per cent of people with a college education, and likewise 31 per cent of people who make monthly payments of over $100 place the cost of installment credit at 6 per cent or under. On the whole, the various population groups have quite similar notions about the cost of installment credit. The one exception perhaps is that, on the average, Negroes place the cost of installment credit higher than whites.*

"The relatively great frequency with which costs of 4 or 5 and especially 6 per cent were mentioned may be interpreted as a carry-over from other information. Especially better educated people dislike to confess to an interviewer that they do not know the answer to a simple question. Other studies conducted a few years ago showed that the rate of in-

---

* William A. Hussong, general manager of the Navy Federal Credit Union explained to the Douglas Committee this apparent contradiction that low income people—and most Negroes fall into this category—are more aware of the cost of debt. "The educated person, while generally proficient in calculations involving rates of simple interest, has difficulty recognizing, let alone analyzing, the perverted rates spawned by the credit industry. On the other hand, the less educated low-income person, because of the frequency of his contact with credit merchants and because the total of his easy payments usually represent a substantial portion of his paycheck, instinctively seems to have a greater awareness of credit cost. In his words, he knows when he is being took but can't say why or for how much."

terest paid on U. S. Government savings bonds is well known (3 per cent or 'about 3 per cent' was the common answer) and the same is true of the interest rate obtained on savings accounts. Most people also know that borrowing costs more than what one gets on savings. On the basis of these pieces of information, some people appear to have surmised an answer to the question of cost of installment buying. They mention some percentages with which they are familiar and which seem appropriate to them. *Actually, their answers are uninformed guesses."* (Italics added.)

The extent of this ignorance afflicts even those who should have at least a minimal comprehension of the cost of debt. Donald J. MacKinnon, treasurer and general manager of the Ford Dearborn Federal Credit Union, testified during Senate hearings on the proposed Douglas consumer credit labeling bill. MacKinnon said that he had attended a lecture at a high school which included a discussion of comparative credit rates. The teacher told the class that $6 per $100 meant 6 per cent simple annual interest. MacKinnon pointed out it is nearly 12 per cent. The teacher, he said, was surprised to learn that it is common for the most respected credit institutions to charge substantially higher rates than the teacher had believed.

The credit union official went on to recall the case of a high-school mathematics teacher of a large city who taught in one of the country's progressive educational systems. This math teacher wrote an article in a professional magazine stating that 1 per cent interest per month equaled 6 per cent per annum simple interest. In fact it is 12 per cent.

Perhaps most startling of all was the testimony given by William McC. Martin Jr., Chairman of the Board of Governors of the Federal Reserve System. An excerpt from the Douglas' hearings follows.

Senator Douglas: Mr. Martin, what do you think is the general thesis on how the rate of interest should be expressed— in annual terms or as a percentage of the outstanding unpaid balance?

Mr. Martin: I will have to be honest with you. It has been confusing to me, on a number of occasions on transactions that I have been involved in to try to figure out just exactly what it is.

Senator Douglas: You mean the present practices are confusing?

Mr. Martin: Not only the present practices are confusing, but how you figure it is confusing . . . I have had very few transactions of this sort. But take an automobile that has fire insurance, burglary insurance, and theft insurance, and other things on it. You trade in an old car, and you try to figure the unpaid balance. The purchaser may be willing to pay for the car *in toto,* you see, but he wants to know what it would cost him if he financed the balance, including the cost of insurance and other charges involved in the use of credit.

Senator Douglas: I think this is very significant testimony because you are probably the most expert man in the field of finance in the United States. In civilian life, you were president of the New York Stock Exchange. You rose to be Assistant Secretary of the Treasury. You have now, for many years, been Chairman of the Board of Governors of the Federal Reserve System. If the present practices are confusing to you, the most expert man in the country, what do you imagine they are to the average workman?

The Senator could as easily have included middle income families. In 1959, more than 75 per cent of all personal debt was owed by consumers with incomes of $4,000 and above. Yet young college educated middle-income families—often the biggest users of credit—are not only possessed by the typical debtor's illusions, but literally pick their own pockets when they buy on time. William H. Whyte Jr.,* writing in *Fortune,* examined the budgets of eighty-three young couples in the $5,000 to $7,500 income bracket. The author observes, "With a few exceptions, the couples reveal themselves as so unconcerned with total cost or interest rates that they provide a veritable syllabus of ways to make two dollars do the work of one." What's more, Whyte notes, the junior executives who someday will help run the nation's economy are not much more prudent than anyone else. "Like the rest of their contemporaries," he says, "in managing their own personal affairs they demonstrate an almost romantic disinterest in money."

The rising young suburbanites' eager acceptance of debt and what happens as a result was dramatically reflected in the experience of the manager of a Long Island small-loan office. The manager recalled how the community in which he was raised and now serves was once the home of clam diggers and potato farmers. The arrival of World War II and the defense plants began turning the area into suburban communities. The potato farmers gradually discovered there was more money to be made in selling their land to developers.

---

* Whyte's article "Budgetism: Opiate of the Middle Class," published in *Fortune,* in May, 1956, is an expanded version of material that appeared in his book, *The Organization Man.* I might add that although there exists a weighty body of literature on the economics of consumer credit, the attempts at social analysis—how debt affects peoples' lives—is comparatively sparse. Hence, my extended quotation from Whyte, one of the few people who has discussed the subject with exceptional understanding and insight.

However, for the young accountants, teachers, electricians and engineers who replaced the Long Island potato farmers their new euphoria comes hard. Their first adventure in suburbia is supported on yearly incomes of between $6,000 and $6,500. Their mortgaged homes are valued at between $13,000 and $19,000. The manager of the small-loan office summed up their condition:

"They lived in apartments all their lives. Most of them in Brooklyn and Queens. Their dream was to leave their second and third generation environments and move into the country. The great American dream. So they come out here and buy homes. And that's when it begins. Although they had enough furniture for their apartments, they cannot fill the houses they bought. They go to the big suburban shopping centers. Within a half hour they've opened two charge accounts in the branch department stores. For the first time they have a plot of ground. They must get grass growing as soon as possible. Another outlay for gardening tools. Then they start commuting. When they lived in Brooklyn, they took the subway and paid thirty cents a day. In suburbia they have to take the Long Island Railroad. This is another thirty or forty dollars a month. By the time a year or year and a half has passed they come to us—to consolidate their debts. This means we lend them money to pay off all their other debts. They have a longer time to pay us back, which cuts down their monthly load." Although the small-loan manager didn't say it, he could have added that debt consolidation also means a higher rate of interest. Depending upon the size of the loan it can be as much as 30 per cent a year in New York State. "I guess," he concluded, "these people just don't know how to handle their new expenses."

The inability to manage their personal finances is a continuing part of the suburban couple's existence. This immersion in debt binds thousands to a protracted life of never-quite-making-ends-meet. One can be sure that if our Puritan ancestors had chosen such an existence there would have been a constant stampede to the rum bottles. William Whyte in his *Fortune* article traces what happens to a family in credit in wonderland by presenting this reasonably typical record of an actual middle-income couple.

Ed Doe, a twenty-nine-year-old cost accountant, earns $6,000. Until recently, he and his wife Mary thought they had an excellent asset-debt position. When they married eight years ago, they were given $1,500 by his parents. Mary continued work as a librarian, they had no children, lived in an apartment, and managed to save $800 in two years. Their first child set them back a little, but even when they moved into their new house—and Mary stopped working—they remained in good shape. The down payment on the house—a $12,000, three-bedroom ranch house—was $2,000 and they still managed to hang on to $300.

Now, like thousands of others in their age group, they are being pinched. A second child and a dinette set absorbed their $300 savings. The roof of their new house has sprung a leak. The wife recently was sick for four weeks, and contrary to their expectations, hospitalization insurance fell far short of covering all the bills. There is still one room virtually unfurnished. Their little girl, now seven, is going to need braces on her teeth.

On the first of the month Ed and Mary don't joke any more about the deductions on Ed's paycheck. It reads, from left to right $500 gross income, $61.80 whdg & FOAB, $4.36 Bl Cross, $17.50 bond ded. Net $416.34.

The next phase is almost as automatic. When Ed sits down at his desk (price, $73.95, on which $14.75 has been paid so far) he writes out an $80 check for the mortgage payment (of which $37.50 is for interest, $15 for taxes and insurance). Next comes a $54 payment to the bank—the fourth of twenty-four monthly payments on a $1,900 car. Then $21 for the monthly premium on a $10,000 straight life policy. (One of these days, Ed reminds himself, he's going to float a loan so he can save 6 per cent by paying the premium annually.) Next: $14.75 for furniture installment loan; $18.30 to the company's credit union for a twenty-four-month $400 loan to pay medical bills; $15 to a department store for the regular "revolving credit" plan payment; $6.18 to the telephone company; $20 to the utility company for heat and light.

This has been the easy part. The Does have only about $190 of their income left to spend, but in this area they are unsupported by the discipline of mandatory payments. Ed has to leave at least $100 in the checking account for food; his wife thinks she usually spends about $80 a month for food, and he will need at least $20 for his own lunches. They are fairly sure about the $16 for the church (this is an untypically heavy commitment) and the $20 or $25 for gas, oil, and car repairs, and the $2.90 for the newspaper boy.

This leaves Ed and Mary with about $45. This must provide for clothing, entertainment, drugstore purchases, cleaning, laundry, a part-time cleaning woman once a week, baby sitter, cigarettes—not to mention any savings for future vacations, gifts, and other seasonal needs. There will not, of course, be enough money. But no matter; the deficit can easily be taken care of by another loan. Ed and Mary are glad they live so conservatively.

Why are couples like Ed and Mary Doe or Alice and Ralph Homer, described in Chapter 1, able to accept and even seek a life of endless debt? Part of the explanation is that our society provides a much greater degree of financial security than our fathers and forefathers enjoyed. Company pension plans, unemployment insurance, social security, group health insurance, all contribute to this feeling of confidence. The specter of the Depression of the nineteen thirties does not haunt the new generation. The built-in safeguards assure them that it can't happen again. The young middle income family has no overwhelming reason to fear continual involvement in debt.

An equally important reason why debt is so eagerly grasped is that without it the Homers could not realize the Twentieth Century American Dream. As the small-loan manager noted earlier, suburbia demands a standard of living which Ralph and Alice desperately want but could not afford without credit. Thus, debt becomes a necessity, even a virtue, and most assuredly a habit. As the Homers move up the suburban social scale and the desires of the family expand, they seek out more debt. Yet, whenever they catch up with the Joneses, the Joneses always refinance. Theirs is an existence where income never matches outgo. For Ralph and Alice Homer the controlling figure in their lives is the bill collector.

Oddly, fear of the omnipresent collector, the shadow that always walks with debt, does not seem to trouble many families. They rarely consider what might happen if they had to face the additional expenses of a personal catastrophe. Nor do they concern themselves with the fact that in effect they have become the bill collector's indentured servant. Finally, they do not seem to understand that loss of a job, illness, a recession, all common occurrences, can easily bring them into a condition of virtual serfdom where everything but their souls is in hock to their creditors. That such circumstances do occur is no exaggeration. One Chicago collection agency reports it has set up an employment service for debtors who can no longer pay their bills. The debtors take on additional jobs so that they can continue to feed their families and still satisfy their creditors. Yet Ralph and Alice merrily roll along, ignorant of the dangers that surround them, blissfully happy in their mortgaged homes, with still-to-be-paid-for-furniture, appliances and cars.

I might add that not everyone is blithely unaware of the cost and dangers of living on time. Recently Mrs. James R. McManus, the wife of a California advertising executive, launched Charge Accounts Anonymous. "C.A.A.," she explained, "is patterned after Alcoholics Anonymous. When a woman has the temptation to go out and charge, she calls a member. We send a friend to talk to her about how much extra a charge account might cost her. Usually, the tempted one abandons the trip."

The Homers, though, have never been introduced to Charge Accounts Anonymous. Indeed, it is questionable as to whether they would recognize its virtues. For Ralph and Alice willingly, even eagerly, accept a life of continuous debt. How, one may wonder, are the Homers able to adjust so easily to this kind of endless servitude? According to Whyte one thing that sustains them is what he calls Budget-itis, where all expenses are measured in monthly payments. Ask a typical suburbanite how much something costs, and his answer may be $12.73 a month. The monthly payment is the only figure the suburbanite feels is relevant. Unless the item is a brand name they are often hazy about the true price. What's more, they purposefully seek to entrap themselves in budgets. For in self-entrapment there is security. As Whyte sums it up: "The suburbanites try to budget so tightly that there will be no unappropriated funds, for they know these would burn a hole in their pockets. Not merely out of greed for goods, then, do they commit themselves. It is protection they want, too; and though it would be extreme to say that they go into debt to be secure, carefully charted debt does give them peace of mind—and in suburbia this is more coveted than luxury itself."

Budgetitis serves another purpose. For the suburban family, indeed for the average consumer, it helps hide the hefty additional sums he pays to live on time. Since the debtor's only interest is the monthly payment, he rarely asks the total cash price, and almost never inquires about the additional cost of credit. But even more important, the time buyer lives in perpetual ignorance, a state of financial illiteracy that is fostered and maintained by the debt merchants. Thus, if the debtor should break his budget bond and attempt to calculate how much he pays for living on time he would be completely incapable of reaching an accurate figure.

The reason why the debt merchants want us to remain credit imbeciles is simple. Credit has become an end in itself. In many instances more profit is derived from credit than from the goods and services being sold. The sums this privilege costs the consumer and the money it brings in to the debt merchant can be astounding. Here are just two examples of what debt cost. The examples were offered in a brochure put out by California's Consumer Counsel.

A store sells a refrigerator for $329.95. On a twenty-four-month contract with a $10 down payment, Mr. Consumer pays the store $66 extra for credit, enough to buy 285 quarts of milk.

Or assume Mr. Consumer wants to buy one of those new compact cars. The cost comes to $2,660.52, including de-luxe accessories, sales tax and license. With a $460.52 down payment, credit charges on the $2,200 balance on a thirty-six-month contract can cost him over $400, enough to purchase a washing machine and dryer.

To understand how these additional costs are hidden from the consumer it will be helpful to examine the debt merchants' methods of calculating carrying or finance charges. What follows is a simplified explanation of credit costs. It will show why the consumer who buys on time is faced with a wonderland of charges. If the different methods of calculating credit costs were understood, consumers might save themselves hundreds of dollars.

There are three methods generally used by credit grantors to calculate the finance charges the consumer pays. The three methods are called add-on, discount, and interest on the unpaid balance.

The add-on method. Here the debt merchant *adds* the finance charge to the amount the customer borrows. For example, if you borrow $100 for one year and the add-on rate is 6 per cent, the total amount you have to pay back is $106. If you repay the money on a monthly basis over a year's time, you pay back $8.83 each month. (To arrive at the $8.83 figure, you simply divide $106 by twelve months.)

The discount method. Here the debt merchant *subtracts* the finance charge from the amount the customer borrows. For example, if you ask for $100 for one year and the discount rate is 6 per cent, the amount you receive is $94. If you repay the money on a monthly basis over a year's time, you pay back $8.33 each month. (To arrive at the $8.33 figure, you simply divide $100 by twelve months.) You will note the total amount you have to repay the lender using the add-on method is $106, of which $100 is the sum you have to spend and $6 is the finance charge. Under the discount method the total amount you will repay is $100, of which $94 is the sum you have to spend and $6 is the finance charge. Thus, under the discount method you pay back less because you borrowed less.

Interest on the unpaid balance. Here the interest or finance charge is calculated each month on the amount you still owe the debt merchant. For example, you borrow $100. Let's assume your first monthly payment is $7. Out of that sum $6 goes to pay back the loan and the remaining $1 is for the finance charge. Thus, on your second payment you would only pay a finance charge on the unpaid balance of $94. The interest or finance charge you pay under the unpaid balance method costs the least, assuming the rate is the same as that for the add-on and discount method. The reason is simple. The interest or finance charge you pay is computed on progressively smaller amounts.

The monthly repayments used in the first two examples point up the fact that figures may have a different meaning than what appears at first glance. Here is the reason. The monthly payment calculated in the *discount method* came to $8.33; for the *add-on method* $8.83, or 50 cents more. It would appear that the finance rate is higher when the add-on method is used. Actually the reverse is true. Under the add-on method you borrowed $100. Under the discount method you borrowed only $94. Yet in both instances you paid the identical finance charge of $6. Thus, on a percentage basis you were charged a higher finance rate under the discount method. In terms of simple annual interest, which I will discuss in a moment, the add-on method in the example given comes to 11.1 per cent; the discount method, approximately 11.8 per cent, or 0.7 per cent more.

The next point is crucial. The only way the consumer can truly compare the cost of credit is through simple annual interest, just mentioned. Before explaining what this means, it is worth noting that this method is used in all fields but consumer credit. All business firms use it when they have to borrow money. The cost to the United States of its bonds and notes is figured in terms of simple annual interest. As Peter Henle, assistant director of research for the AFL-CIO, noted, "In fact, when the sales finance companies have to go to the bond market to raise funds, the interest rate for any issue of their securities is expressed in terms of simple annual interest." For the consumer, an understanding of simple annual interest and how it works is a must. It is the only yardstick he can use to compare the cost of credit.

By definition, true or simple annual interest is the amount paid for the use of money for one year. It is always stated as a percentage. The essential point to understand is this: simple annual interest on money to be repaid over a year's time is generally double the rate the debt merchant quotes to the consumer.

A simple case. You borrow $100. Your finance charge is calculated under the add-on method at 10 per cent. Thus, your finance charge comes to $10. You agree to pay back the sum you borrowed on a monthly basis over a year's time. This means— and this is the key point—you will not have the entire $100 for a full year. Remember you are continually paying back one-twelfth of what you borrowed each month. Thus, as the months go by, you have the use of progressively smaller amounts of money. If you average the amount out you will find that you actually have the use of approximately one-half of the $100 you borrowed or about

$50 for the entire year.* This means that the $10 finance charge you are paying must be applied against $50—the amount you actually have to use—and not $100. Stated in terms of simple annual interest this comes to approximately 20 per cent ($50, the sum you have to use divided into $10, the finance charge.)

One further point. The time factor in calculating interest is of extreme importance. You will note in the above example the sum borrowed was for an entire year. What happens, however, if you should borrow a certain amount for less than a year? How does this shorter time period affect your calculation of true annual interest, which by definition is the amount paid for the use of money for one year?

Take this example. You purchase a $10 item. The finance charge comes to $1, which you pay immediately. You agree to repay the remaining $10 at the rate of $1 a week for ten weeks. In terms of simple annual interest, the finance charge comes to 104 per cent. Here is why. Let us assume you had taken a full year to repay the $10 debt. Now, the debt merchant is charging you $1 for ten weeks. For twenty weeks, he would charge you $2. For one year he would charge you $5.20 (5.2 times $1, the ten-week finance charge.) From the previous example you will recall that during the period of a year you had use of only half the sum you borrowed. Thus, over the entire year you would have use of $5, not $10, the original amount of your debt. Stated in terms of simple annual interest this comes to 104 per cent ($5, the sum you have to use, divided into $5.20, the finance charge you would pay over a year's time equals 104 per cent).†

* When you average the amount you actually have to use over the year it always comes out to a little more than half of the total sum you borrowed.
† Please note appendix for formula that may be used to calculate the true annual interest.

In the wonderland of credit, however, the consumer is almost never told the cost of debt in terms of true annual interest. Thus, it is virtually impossible for him to know whether he is paying exorbitant sums for the use of credit. For example, the price of credit frequently varies among merchants who sell identical merchandise. But the way these finance plans are presented it is often difficult for people to tell which plan is more costly. Take just two instances. New car financing in unregulated states may range from 12 to 120 per cent true annual interest. The cost of revolving credit within the same department store may vary from 18 to 80 per cent.

There is another way of showing the marked variations in the cost of credit. Let's assume Ralph and Alice Homer decide to buy a bed. Depending upon the source from which they buy or borrow on time within their own community, the price they pay for credit may vary considerably. Here are just a few of the things that can happen:

1. The Homers decide to deal with a high pressure credit furniture store where they pay a 10 per cent fee for the privilege of repaying the money in three monthly installments. Their true annual interest rate will amount to about 60 per cent.

2. They can borrow the money from a small-loan company to make the purchase. Depending upon state law they may pay 3 per cent on the unpaid balance or a true annual interest rate of 36 per cent.

3. The Homers can make their purchase through a department store or mail-order house and pay 1½ per cent a month on the declining balance or 18 per cent true annual interest. (If the Homers, while shopping at the mail-order house, should spend less than $100 per item for a number of

items their charges may amount to as much as 40 per cent. The charge in this case will be listed as a $5 carrying charge for $50 worth of merchandise for six months.)

4. Ralph or Alice Homer can borrow the money from their credit union and pay 1 per cent a month on the unpaid balance or a true annual interest of 12 per cent.

5. Ralph Homer can borrow the money through the personal loan department of his bank. The cost will be advertised at 6 to 9 per cent. In terms of true annual interest the rates will run 12 to 18 per cent.

6. Finally, Ralph Homer, if he has collateral, may be able to get a single payment loan for 6 to 8 per cent true annual interest. Some banks, however, are not interested in such rates controlled by state usury laws. Instead, the bank might encourage Ralph Homer to open a check credit account at true annual interest rates from 18 to 24 per cent or direct him to the personal loan department where he will pay from 12 to 18 per cent for an installment personal loan.

Unfortunately, neither the Homers nor the vast majority of consumers could hope to calculate the cost of most credit, since it is conveniently hidden by a myriad of rates, figures and methods. For example, the consumer may be quoted the discount or add-on rate. The add-on rate is usually used in the sale of cars on credit. But the consumer is almost never told that the true interest is about double the discount or add-on rate. In fact, back in 1941 the Federal Trade Commission ruled that the "add-on" rate is misleading. This decision was upheld by the federal courts. Said the courts in upholding the Commission: "The average individual does not make, and often is incapable of making, minute calculations to the term and the cost of property purchased on the deferred payment plan." However, despite the F.T.C.'s ruling and the judicial decision, credit grantors continue to offer the add-on rate without any meaningful explanation.

Another way the cost of credit is disguised is where the price of credit is quoted as a monthly rate figured on the unpaid balance, a typical practice of small-loan companies. Actually, the true annual rate is twelve times the quoted monthly rate.* When Mrs. Consumer opens a revolving credit account at her favorite department store, all she is told is that she will pay a service charge of 1½ per cent a month on the unpaid balance. The true annual interest rate? Roughly 18 per cent. Indeed, it can come to much more, as pointed out by John F. Doyle, supervisor of the Division of Consumer Credit, State Banking Department of Wisconsin. Writing in the Spring, 1958 issue of the *Personal Finance Law Quarterly Report,* Doyle came up with this astounding discovery:

"At the time the department began investigating revolving credit," Doyle wrote, "they found that the merchandise purchased in all instances was not being used for a full month. Consequently, when the charge of 1½ per cent was added at the beginning of the month on the balance outstanding at the end of the previous month, it gave a much larger yield than 18 per cent per annum. For instance, if the purchase was made on the last day of the month and the accounts billed on the following day, the yield [for the first payment] would not be 18 per cent per annum, but *540 per cent on the basis of the merchandise sold.* If you are to take into consideration a yield on the cost of the mer-

---

* This does NOT mean that a charge on a $100 loan at 2½ per cent a month repaid in twelve equal monthly installments (which comes to 30 per cent simple annual interest) is $30. Actually it is $17 because the 2½ per cent is being calculated on the unpaid balance, which each month becomes progressively smaller.

chandise, and consider that there might be a 100 per cent markup, then the department store is getting an interest yield of *1040 per cent per year.*" (Italics added.)

Perhaps the worst abuses are "easy terms" or "easy payment" plans. Here, even a mathematical genius couldn't calculate the cost of credit. Although the ads tell the consumer that he will pay so much down, so much a month, they frequently do not say how many months the payment is going to continue. Nor is the price of credit listed. One of my favorites contains this series of persuasive admonitions:

> PLEASE
> *DO NOT* Bring Any Money
> *DO NOT* Bring Any Co-Signers
> *DO NOT* Own Any Property
> *JUST* Have a Steady Job

The consumer is then given a choice of twenty-six cars, each to be purchased for so much per week (not month). No mention is made of a down payment, the cost of the credit, or how long the payments will last. The top of the ad carries this ironic headline: "NEW CREDIT REGULATIONS PASSED AT (XYZ) MOTOR CO." Avertisements similar to this appear in newspapers daily. In fact, just for the fun of it, check today's paper and try to find the ad that includes the cost of credit. This exercise should point up a simple truth. Easy credit isn't easy.

In the spring of 1960 readers of *The New York Times* and other papers were startled by a most unusual full page ad. Paid for by the Bowery Savings Bank, the largest savings bank in the country, the advertisement's theme was: what would happen to the subway user's pocketbook if he decided to ride now and pay later. It showed in simplest terms how to figure the additional costs of buying subway tokens on time. The purpose of the ad, of course, was to get people to keep their credit purchases at a minimum and deposit their extra cash in the Bowery Savings Bank. However, the ad did show that the credit costs can be expressed clearly and simply in terms of true annual interest. It also served another function. Except for educational programs carried out by credit unions and some labor unions, it was one of the rare times that the consumer was shown the true cost of credit.

There actually is a program in existence whose aim is to help the young consumer of high school and college age understand the intricacies of credit. Accepted by numerous authorities it is widespread in its use. In my opinion, however, instead of clarifying and explaining the cost of credit, it virtually promotes debtor confusion.

This program began in 1956 under the aegis of the National Foundation for Consumer Credit. By its own claims, the Foundation, located in the nation's capital, is a non-profit research and educational organization. Its sponsors include large and small manufacturers, wholesale distributors, retailers, banks, consumer and commercial finance companies and insurance companies throughout the United States and Canada. A partial list of its fifty-three board of directors members for 1959-60 includes: Vice Adm. E. Dorsey Foster (USN retired), vice president of Radio Corporation of America; William A. Lank, president of the Farmers National Bank, Bloomsburg, Pa.; Ralph N. Larson, president of the Morris Plan Co. of California; De Witt J. Paul, senior vice president, Beneficial Management Corp.; Frank J. Ross, general credit manager of Sears, Roebuck & Co.; Richard C. Sachs, president of Sachs Quality Stores, New York.

The Foundation's stated aims are: "To bring to consumers

a complete continuing study of every phase of Consumer Credit; *sound programs of education for intelligent, safe use of credit by the people;* a modernized, better credit service." Perhaps the Foundation's most successful effort to date is a fifty-four-page booklet entitled, "Using Our Credit Intelligently." Written by William J. Cheyney, executive vice president of the Foundation, the text was studied by more than fifty teachers, superintendents and principals. It had been checked by the Home Economics, Social Studies and Vocational Training Divisions of the Office of Education of the U. S. Department of Health, Education and Welfare. Finally, it was favorably reviewed by nearly all State Departments of Education and the Federal Extension Service of the U. S. Department of Agriculture. Now in its third printing, the Foundation's book is being used by high schools in more than 1,300 cities throughout the country. It has been approved by the school authorities in Chicago, Boston, New York, Washington, D. C., Baltimore, Philadelphia, San Francisco, Kansas City, Indianapolis and the entire state of Louisiana, among others. In addition, it is used in forty colleges and universities, including the universities of Illinois, California, Texas, Cornell and Ohio State. It is fast becoming one of the more popular items used to tutor American youth.

It must be noted that "Using Our Credit Intelligently" does advise its young readers not to overload themselves with debt. It also points out that the shorter the term of payments, the smaller the credit cost. And it mentions organizations like the Better Business Bureau and warns you never to go into hiding when "an emergency makes some change in the payment plan absolutely necessary."

Despite the approval of the authorities, as one reads it one becomes aware that this little booklet with its profusion of two-color illustrations has all the gloss of the soft sell. A threnody to on-the-cuff living, it stresses the virtues of Budgetitis. While it tells the future Ralph and Alice Homers that they should meet their monthly payments, it does not tell them that they are often being overcharged. Nor does it offer its young readers a true understanding of the cost of credit. The figures used in many of the examples are considerably lower than the percentages encountered by the actual time customer. Though simple annual interest is described, it is included as only one of a variety of methods to calculate finance charges. Indeed, no attempt is made to show that this is the only yardstick which the consumer can use to compare the various costs of credit. William J. Cheyney, the author, offered this interesting explanation during his appearance before the Douglas Committee:

"In this unit, we have not insisted upon disclosure in the terms of a simple interest rate per annum. The educational authorities with whom we have worked, have not requested this . . . As to the newer forms of revolving credit in both cash lending and retailing, our unit has made every effort to see that the public clearly understands the nature and amount of all charges there assessed. We believe the current practice to express revolving credit charges as a simple addition of a percentage of the outstanding balance each month is readily understood, but that *to convert this expression to an annual rate at simple interest would confuse and frighten far more people than ever will be clarified by this procedure.*" (Italics added.)

It would appear that if our children are to be properly taught the meaning and cost of debt living, their education should be based on a program sponsored by a representative consumers group. Certainly, one may earnestly question the propriety of our public schools using material inspired by those who would profit most from the sale of credit, the debt merchants themselves.

7 *The Pied Pipers of Debt*

> To quote Bernice Fitz-Gibbon again: "Cast your
> bread upon the daughters, not upon the mothers
> and grandmothers, for the daughters (and I add the
> sons too) are the future of your business." And we
> might paraphrase that to say, "Cast your credit upon
> the daughters."
>
> *From a speech by Kay Corinth, merchandise
> director,* Seventeen Magazine.

Item: A disc jockey in Lancaster, Pennsylvania, tempts his
teen-age listeners with this offer: Each youngster receives
a free 45 L.P. record of a hit song. All the child has to do is
request an application to join a local department store's new
program—a teen-age credit account.

Item: In Kansas City, Missouri, a credit manager unhappily announced his store only had 120 teen-age credit
accounts. Their total charges came to a meager $3,100. He
added ruefully, "We had a couple of accounts that bought
nothing but candy."

Item: One merchant sells his on-the-cuff living to teen-
agers by promoting the plan with local school authorities
and the Parent-Teachers Association. When the youngster
joins the plan he receives a white honor charge card with
the credit limit set at $25. If all goes well at the end of the
first year he is given a silver charge card. At the end of the
second year the teen-ager receives a gold card, he's recom-

mended to the local credit bureau, and his limit is raised to $50. And all this can be accomplished without parental authority of any kind. Among the boons of living on time even our children can win status through debt.

For the debt merchant teen-age credit promises new vistas of wealth. When the exponents of credit for children contemplate this cornucopia of riches, they manage to achieve a rare glow. One of the most forceful is Kay Corinth, merchandise director of *Seventeen Magazine,* which claims to reach one-third of all female teen-agers in the United States. As the magazine's merchandise director, Kay Corinth is an expert on the potentials of childhood. Here is an excerpt from a speech she made in 1959 before the Credit Management Division of the National Retail Merchants Association. This portion is simply titled: "THEIR MONEY."

O.K., so we have more customers from the teen-age market. (An estimated twenty-seven million by 1967.) But how about the "dough" they have to spend? Are they worth the expense of carrying their accounts? That's what we're really interested in. Bernice Fitz-Gibbon, advertising's greatest woman, coined a wonderful phrase when she named them the "Teen Tycoons, because they are so rich!"

A moment ago I told you that 39 per cent of all teen-age girls work, and they earn 2.6 billion dollars. With what this group earns, plus allowances from families, the dollar figure on the female side of the market is 4.2 billion dollars! Add to that gift money, blank checks from father, and using mother's charga-plate when daughter doesn't have her own.

The market potential of both boys and girls is at least ten billion dollars, Kay Corinth adds. By 1967, it should reach fifteen billion.

In their effort to partake of these childhood riches, some debt merchants have actually set up credit plans for twelve- and thirteen-year-olds. An apparel store in Kilmarnock, Virginia, grants credit to children still in junior high school. The maximum limit is set at $12 with a minimum payment of one dollar a week. The $12 limit, however, is comparatively low. Most stores which offer teen-age credit permit children to charge between $25 and $50, and a few have fixed the limit as high as $120. Occasionally a youngster will run berserk and shoot his account up to $150. He is able to do this because some stores allow teen-age time purchases without a floor release limit or sales authorization. Furthermore, even though almost all stores have predetermined limits as to the amount youngsters can charge, revolving credit, the plan most frequently offered, can keep teen-agers in perpetual debt if they continue to charge new purchases before the old purchases have been paid up.

Although no one knows precisely how many department and specialty stores offer teen-age credit, the number is rapidly increasing. According to a *Seventeen Magazine* survey of 217 stores, 64 per cent had some form of credit for teen-agers. A similar study made a year earlier (in 1959) put the figure at 32 per cent. The current survey also notes that in the consumer credit explosion of the last decade, the teen-age fuse is only a recent addition. Although two far-sighted debt merchants offered special credit plans for Teen Tycoons as early as 1954 and 1955, some 58 per cent began their programs as late as 1959. The survey also notes that debt for teen-agers is not only catching on with the stores but the youngsters themselves. By the spring of 1960, 58 per cent of the stores with special teen plans had up to 250 active accounts. In 1959, the survey added, 49 per cent of the stores had one hundred or less accounts on their books. Finally by March 1960 seven stores could claim between five hundred and eleven-hundred youngsters on their rosters. And one store said it had sold fourteen hundred children on its buy-now, pay-later plans.

/ One of the unusual aspects of teen-age credit is that, unlike adult debt, the credit grantor in most instances has no way of forcing teen-agers to pay up. In almost all states the law says that if goods are sold to an infant, usually defined as anyone under twenty-one,* the infant may renege on the contract at any time before reaching his legal adulthood or within a reasonable time thereafter. Although merchandise sold to a teen-ager may be repossessed, he is not legally responsible if the goods are squandered.) All of which means Junior can smash his time-bought Elvis Presley records and not worry about the sheriff. Some stores try to get around this by asking parents to guarantee their youngsters' accounts. The vast majority, however, simply take the risk. Since the teen-age credit volume at this point is relatively small, the loss potential is minimal. Also most teen-agers pay up. For the few who do not, the pressure usually used is the invariable threat that Junior is besmirching his credit character. But if Junior persists in being a dead beat, he usually is charged off to profit and loss.

Some debt merchants, though, do not give up so easily. One credit manager, for example, calls on the parents and informs them that unless they pay their child's overdue bills their youngsters will be publicly exposed in court. If the

---

* In at least nine states females reach their majority at eighteen. And in at least six states both boys and girls are legally considered grownups as soon as they marry, which means the bill collector can garnishee a married teen-ager's wages or put a lien on his allowance.

parents insist that legally he has no case, the credit manager replies: "I know we can't win. But do you want your kid to have a court record?"

One problem credit managers have had to solve was the criteria they could use for deciding whether Junior would be a good risk. Many teen-agers hold part-time or full-time jobs. This means that youngsters can fulfill two of the three C's, Capital and Capacity. But how to judge the third C, Credit Character? Since nearly all teen-agers have yet to build a credit dossier, the debt merchants searched elsewhere. As the manager of one medium-sized department store put it:

"If the parents show a good credit record, we take a chance on the children. If their record is bad, then the child's record will be bad. That doesn't mean we reject all kids whose parents have bad histories. Why, we might take a chance on a youngster if he has a good part-time job and seems to understand something about credit. I would say our teen-age rejection rate is between two and three per cent. It's always because their parents are bad risks. Although we don't tell the kids why we reject them, they know it's because their parents owe a lot of money."

In the inexorable logic of the debt merchant, there are families like the Jukes and the Kallikaks who pass on their credit sins from generation to generation. One might question whether the rejected teen-ager always knows his parents are looked upon as credit bums. And one may further wonder, if he does know, whether this is the healthy way to handle children. It appears that if such thoughts disturb some debt merchants, their conscience has been successfully tranquilized by "all that beautiful green money" in the hands of those Teen Tycoons.

Since teen-age debt is so recent an innovation, credit managers are still experimenting with the solutions to two problems: How do we entice the community's children to become full-time debtors? The kids might go for it, but will their parents? In her speech *Seventeen*'s Kay Corinth had no trouble in offering solutions to the first problem. Here are five steps in her ten-step program for bringing teenagers into credit plans. All, I might add, have been used effectively by the Pied Pipers of debt.

1. Plan an educational program with the launching of your plan. Contact your local board of education and invite them to bring classes to your store for lessons or "labs" in credit, and what it means and how to use it. As a part of your talk to students, explain your junior plan. Schools are receptive to such classes if you are uncommercial. The credit you have to sell must be purely the "for instance" of the lesson.

2. Ask your publicity department to serve all local papers, including school papers, with the story of your new credit offering. They might even have a press conference for editors of school papers.

3. Give the program a special promotional name—one that will designate it as an account for juniors. Don't use the word "teen" in the name, as these customers think of themselves as young juniors.

4. Design special application forms that use the name and that are attractive and friendly. Teens love quiz games, so make it appealing and not frightening. Be sure to ask age so that as they reach the top age-limit you may convert them to regular accounts.

5. Promote . . . promote . . . promote. Young people are the greatest communicators, so use direct mail to reach them. Use newspaper advertising in your local papers, especially in the school papers . . . Use a bill enclosure directed to

parents to tell them the advantage of such an account for their youngsters. . . .

As Kay Corinth summed it up: "Our favorite saying at *Seventeen* is that it's easier to start a habit than to stop one. So start the credit habit in your store with your young customers."

While selling debt to youngsters, the credit managers are convincing parents that "the credit habit" is good for their children. As one credit manager said, it gives "young adults an early education in how to use credit, planning purchases, and assuming responsibility." Another has called teen-age credit "living educational programs in money management." Said a third: "Its purpose is . . . to promote their early appreciation of a good credit standing in their community." To sum up, teen-age credit is not a business but a "community" service. But is it?

Perhaps one could find childhood debt justifiable if it taught youngsters the true cost of credit. But this lesson is ignored in the debt merchants' appeal to both parents and children. For example, all that one program tells its young customers is: "The terms will be two dollars weekly plus a small service charge to be paid for from their own allowance or earnings." Not even a monthly percentage is quoted. Not only is it impossible for youngsters to calculate the true annual interest rates but the service charges are frequently greater than the charges applied against adult accounts.

As noted earlier, revolving credit is the plan most frequently used in teen-age time buying. The service charge for revolving credit usually amounts to 1½ per cent a month, or 18 per cent true annual interest in a year. However, several states have passed legislation that permits minimum charges far in excess of 18 per cent. The minimum charges apply when the ceiling rate of 1½ per cent per month yields less than a certain amount. This means that since many teen-age accounts cannot rise above $25, the teen-ager must pay the higher rates. *Consumer Reports* observed:

"In New York State, for example, the legal minimum charge is 70 cents a month. At that rate, a Junior Account of $25 would cost $8.40 a year in carrying charges; that's 33.6 per cent in true-annual-interest terms. In Colorado the legal minimum is $10 a year, a 40 per cent charge. In California and Florida the legal minimum is $1.00 a month. This comes out to $12 a year, or 48 per cent in true annual interest for such an account. In Kansas the minimum is $15, or 60 per cent at true annual interest. And in Montana the legal minimum is a generous $20 a year; on a $25 teen-age account that amounts to an interest charge of 80 per cent."

One wonders whether parents would be so agreeable in allowing their children to get the debt habit if they knew their youngsters paid out of their own pockets a tuition of between 33 and 80 per cent for their credit education. But the debt merchants are not concerned with a parent rebellion, since neither the parents nor their children could have the vaguest idea that such exorbitant charges are being made. Perhaps the debt merchants' cynicism was best summed up by a credit manager who was asked whether he thought teen-age credit was truly a "community service." The credit manager snapped, "Don't be naïve. We don't do anything for nothing."

Among themselves the debt merchants are equally candid. The manager of one of the Midwest's largest stores wrote in *Credit World,* the credit industry's magazine: "With such a market, we, as credit executives, must do everything in our power to garner for our respective firms our rightful share of this lucrative market, and also through such programs weld the future homemakers of America to our establishments." (Teen-age debt not only builds store loyalty for the present and future but helps addict the teen-ager to the credit habit.)

Despite the surge of teen-age credit, a number of credit managers frown on the whole dismal program. One offered me this somewhat personal explanation: "I have a fifteen-year-old daughter. And I don't think thirteen-, fourteen- and fifteen-year-olds are ready for this sort of thing. They don't have the money and they don't have the sense of responsibility. You have to do some very clear thinking on saving five dollars a month."

Another reassuring answer came from the manager of a collegiate clothing store in California. He had advertised the credit plan in the local college newspapers, but the plan met with little success. He then asked a professor at the college to show the ad to his class and find out why he had failed. One half of the students said they considered the plan just another gimmick to sell them merchandise through debt.

Despite the credit manager with a conscience and the perceptive college students, the Pied Pipers of debt and the army of children that follows them are increasing.

8 *From Kimonos to Instant Money*

It seems that a bright young salesman was trying to
sell an electric dishwasher to a housewife. "Madam,"
he said, "If you buy this dishwasher it will help you
save the cost of a maid. You will be saving every
month."

The housewife hesitated. "Well, I am not sure we
can buy it. We bought an automobile to save bus
fare. Then we bought a television set to save movie
expense. Last week we bought a clothes washer to
save laundry bills. You know, mister, I think we are
saving as much now as we can save."

*Homer J. Livingston, Chicago bank president,
as quoted in* Fortune.

Isaac Merritt Singer, until he reached middle age, was a
magnificent failure. A mechanic and actor, he was spectacu-
larly unsuccessful at both. Vain and argumentative, Singer
quickly quarreled with almost anyone who opposed his will.
It seemed his only talent was siring offspring. Over the years
he managed to beget twenty-four children, in and out of
wedlock. But Singer was to make one other contribution
which changed the lives of millions. As one of the founders
of the sewing machine company that bears his name, Singer
was the first to offer installment buying on a mass scale.
Isaac Merritt Singer's plan not only has had a profound
effect on the American economy, but throughout the world.

It was in 1850, eleven years before the Civil War, that
Singer joined with two other men in the manufacture of
sewing machines. Their working capital totaled $40. Within
a year, Singer not only dominated the company, but the

market. He organized the Sewing Machine Combination, America's first patent pool. Meanwhile, Singer introduced its famous "turtle back" sewing machine for home use. It wasn't long before Singer was caught in a quandary. The "turtle back" model, Singer's cheapest home machine, sold for $125. The average annual income of the American family at that time was $500. Thus, only a few families could afford the necessary cash outlay. Singer solved the problem in 1856 by introducing "hire purchase," another term for installment buying still used in England. Under the Singer plan the customer paid $5 down and $5 a month. Within a year Singer's sales had tripled. By 1874 the firm was selling more machines than those sold by all of its seventeen American competitors. Singer had discovered his own genius and America had found the genie of credit.

Today, thanks to time buying, there are more sewing machines in the United States than telephones, and most of them are Singers. Over fifty-two million women make part of their own draperies, slip covers and dresses.

Even more startling was Singer's campaign to sell sewing machines throughout the world on time. One of the more formidable problems faced by Singer salesmen occurred in Indo-China. Collections of payments were made difficult because the natives frequently moved from village to village. To insure that they would be recompensed, Singer salesmen insisted their sales be guaranteed, usually by someone with a settled business or a village elder. To prove identification, the salesmen would photograph the village elder and customer, with the customer holding a blackboard on which was chalked the number of the machine. For the customer who was illiterate and couldn't sign his name to a contract, the Singer salesman simply took his fingerprints.

Perhaps Singer's greatest triumph was the introduction of its machines and time buying in Japan. Shortly after Commodore Perry opened Japan to American trade, Singer went in with its machines. But this time the company was faced with a problem that seemed at first insuperable. The Japanese kimono, worn by both men and women, was sewed together by loosely basted stitches. To launder it, the kimono had to be taken apart, washed and dried and then sewed together again. For Singer there was one hitch. Their machines only sewed tight stitches, suitable for Western clothes but not kimonos. Singer proceeded to turn out a new machine which could sew a quarter-inch basting stitch. But the Japanese were still unimpressed.

There was one other solution. The Japanese would have to give up their ancient form of dress for the stiff suits and complicated apparel of the West. Singer began a massive campaign to revolutionize Japanese clothes. Its first step was to enlist the aid of Marquis Okuma, one of the last elder statesmen of Japan. With his encouragement, the company set up a huge sewing school in Tokyo that enrolled one thousand day pupils and five hundred boarders. The school offered a three-year course in machine sewing, using the latest Western styles as models. Upon graduation the Japanese seamstresses were given jobs as demonstrators. Similar campaigns were promoted throughout the country.

But Singer didn't stop there. It was the rare Japanese that owned a chair. This left the sewing machine company with the bleak prospect of only being able to sell its hand model, which could be worked on the floor. So began another unrelenting campaign that sang the virtues of Singer's treadle sewing machine, which, of course, could be bought on time. Today many Japanese homes have only one chair, stationed next to the sewing machine. There are now over 1,500,000 Singer machines in Japan alone. Isaac Merritt Singer, a wastrel seemingly destined to failure, not only helped revolutionize the mores of the Orient, but the economy of much of the world.

Although it took a number of years before installment credit caught on, its current importance can be measured in the figures for consumer debt in the United States in 1960. Of the approximately $56 billion owed at the end of that year, nearly $43 billion or about 80 per cent of all consumer debt resulted from installment credit. To put it another way, if the total consumer installment debt was divided by the country's population, every man, woman and child would have owed over $195. By the end of 1959 there were over forty-three million passenger cars in the United States owned by individuals. It is estimated that some twenty-nine million were bought on some kind of installment plan. In the same year, time payments resulted in the sale of 2¾ million television sets, over 1½ million refrigerators and more than two million washing machines. Advancing credit to the consumer has probably resulted in the movement of more goods to more people than any other method of distribution in a free enterprise economy.

In recent years, however, this primary function of consumer credit has undergone a drastic and contradictory change. To put it simply: the original purpose of credit was to sell merchandise and services. Today, the sale of credit has become in many instances an end in itself. Merchandise and services are fast becoming just a tool to sell debt. In fact, it has reached the point where frequently the finance charges actually bring in more profit than the money made on the sale of the goods themselves. Although many debt merchants hesitate to admit it, this startling development occasionally creeps into public print.

Recently the *Wall Street Journal* recorded the remarks of a leading merchandiser of men's wear who began instituting service charges on credit accounts in 1954. According to the clothing merchant his firm in recent years "has earned as much money from service charges on credit accounts as we have in our normal cash business. It's a source of income clothing merchants are foolish to ignore."

Also recorded in the *Wall Street Journal* were the auto industry profit estimates for the first quarter of 1960. The estimates showed that out of the dealers' average profit of $70 per new car, $43 came from the financing charges.

Forbes Magazine informed its readers that R. C. Rolfing of Wurlitzer has learned to make money from financing installment purchases of organs and the like. In 1957, Rolfing formed the Wurlitzer Acceptance Corporation. *Forbes* offers this exuberant quote from the Wurlitzer official: "We are making almost as much money from our financing business as we do from manufacturing and selling."

Wurlitzer is not alone in setting up what the credit industry itself calls captive finance companies. These companies, subsidiaries of large manufacturing retail concerns, are in the business of financing installment sales of their parent firms' products. The boom in captive finance companies started in 1950 when the consumer credit explosion got under way. The range of firms that have set up captive finance companies include Admiral Corporation, manufacturer of television sets and appliances, Armstrong Cork Company, which makes floor and wall coverings, and Montgomery Ward & Company. Their aim is twofold: To help finance their dealers and thus move goods, and to reap the sizable profits that come from selling credit. A. W. Bernsonn, managing director of the National Appliance and Radio-TV Dealers Association put it bluntly: "In many cases there is more profit at the retail level in the financing than in the sale of the merchandise."

Even the nation's most conservative business institutions are using merchandise as a tool to sell credit. William Whyte Jr., writing in *Fortune,* notes that some department stores are making more profit on the interest charges on revolving credit than they are on the goods themselves. The most hardened credit men are flabbergasted, he says, adding: "Department-store people don't quite have a guilty conscience on the subject, but when they start talking about high administrative overhead, the service to the customer, etc., only the humorless can keep a straight face." He goes on to quote one department store executive, who after closing the door, said: "It's fantastic. Eighteen per cent a year! Imagine it. We didn't expect they would all stay bought up, but if you want to know whether we like the plan, just ask us if we like money."

Revolving credit, the most revolutionary credit discovery since Singer's installment plan, has become a means that bridges both the old and new concept of debt merchandising. It both helps to sell more merchandise and serves as a unique method of selling debt itself. Revolving credit is not only being used by department stores, but by some of the nation's largest banks and even by one of the biggest small-loan companies. As a method of selling debt it may eventually have no competitor.

Revolving credit first came into use in 1938 when Wanamaker and several other department stores tried it. In 1955 the original revolving credit plan was liberalized. This new plan is now known as the all-purpose or option account and can be used either as a revolving credit plan or a thirty-day charge account.

The revolving credit part of the new plan works this way. Alice Homer visits a department store's credit office. Alice and the store's credit representative discuss how much Alice thinks she can afford in monthly payments. Alice says she can pay out $50 a month. The credit representative tells Alice she will be allowed to pay for the merchandise she buys on credit over a six-month period. This means she will be permitted to charge up to $300 in purchases (six monthly payments times $50 equals $300). During the first month Alice charges $300 worth of merchandise. She will then be obligated to pay $50 a month for six months. However, as soon as the store receives Alice's first $50 payment, it will allow her to purchase an additional $50 worth of merchandise on credit. Alice, of course, may charge less than the $300 limit. If she does, her monthly payments will be smaller. Under the revolving credit plan just described, Alice also will pay a service charge of 1½ per cent a month on the unpaid balance or 18 per cent true annual interest a year.

Besides the revolving credit plan in the all-purpose or option account, Alice may, if she chooses, use the thirty-day charge account feature. This permits Alice to pay her total bill within thirty days. By doing so, she will avoid the service charge. Roughly 90 per cent of all department stores offer some form of revolving credit.

Employment of the latest techniques in time buying are not only increasing the sales of department stores, but of the mail-order houses as well. Mail-order sales on credit made by the four largest houses in the field totaled an estimated $412 million in 1950. Just nine years later total credit sales soared

to $852 million, more than double the amount. Sears Roe-
buck, the giant in the field, accounted for $541 million in
credit mail-order sales in 1959 alone. What's more, the mail-
order houses are joining the department stores in the inva-
sion of suburbia. From 1950 to 1960 the number of catalog
stores and telephone offices increased from 777 to 1,731,
many of them located within the burgeoning suburban communities. At these stores a mail-order customer may examine the goods described in the catalogs and within twenty-
four hours he can receive the merchandise shipped from
warehouses scattered throughout the country. Depending
upon the company he may have as many as twenty to twenty-
four months to pay. On mail-order revolving credit, the interest again is 1½ per cent a month on the declining balance
or 18 per cent true annual interest.

Perhaps the most interesting development of all is the
emergence of some of the nation's great commercial banks in
a field that would seem the private preserves of the country's
retailers. Nearly a hundred banks have already cut into
the revolving credit pie. Here one finds in its most distinct
form the blending of the new concept of credit with the old.
The merchants who join the plans offered by the banks aim
to sell merchandise through credit. For the banks, though,
merchandise has simply become a tool to sell debt.

The bank charge account plan was started by a small institution, the Franklin Bank of Long Island, in 1952. But it
wasn't until 1958 when New York's Chase Manhattan and
California's Bank of America decided to try their own plans
that the bank charge account idea took hold. The cost of getting such programs under way can be expensive, even for
banks. The Bank of America, for example, spent some two
million dollars for advertising and promotion during the first

year. An additional $200,000 had to be charged off for renting and purchasing office and accounting equipment to handle the program. In addition, the California institution had to set up a department employing four hundred people to oversee its new Bankamericard operation. Many bankers feel that this is money well spent.

Not only are banks making the plunge, but even a small-loan company has entered the field. Seaboard Finance, the third largest consumer finance company in the nation, launched its International Charge plan in Hawaii in March, 1959. Just one year later the plan was operating in seventeen states and in two Canadian provinces. As of March 31, 1960, account balances totaled over 14½ million dollars with more than 118,000 International Charge credit cardholders.

(The bank charge plans are a marriage of the credit-card idea and department store revolving credit plans. The Chase Manhattan Bank Charge Plan, known to New Yorkers as CMCP, is typical. It works like this: There are over five thousand merchants, many with more than one branch store, who have joined CMCP. Each merchant pays the bank a $25 entrance fee for each store location. He also pays the bank 6 per cent on all CMCP charge sales, but is entitled to have some of that money refunded if his volume is high enough. Like the all-purpose credit-card companies, the bank guarantees all accounts and does all the collection work. For the merchant the profits generally come from the additional sale of merchandise.)

The consumer pays nothing to join the plan. If he passes the CMCP credit check, he receives a credit card, similar to the cards issued by the all-purpose credit-card companies. He also is given a directory that lists the member stores. In addition, the consumer may apply for credit privileges usually ranging from $100 to $500, but may even ask for more. Once he has received his CMCP card he simply presents it at any of the member stores in lieu of cash. At the end of the month he receives one bill with all the sales slips for purchases made during that period. If he pays his bill within twenty days, there is no charge. However, if he chooses he may pay one-twelfth of his bill each month. For this he will be charged 1 per cent on the unpaid balance or 12 per cent true annual interest. For the bank the profit comes through the credit charges to the consumers and the commissions from the merchants. Thus in most plans the banks receive roughly 6 per cent from the retailer, plus 12 to 18 per cent from the consumer.

But this isn't the only profit for banker debt merchants. *Consumer Reports* put it this way: "The seller of debt, like any other seller, has to line up customers. It is here that the shrewd method lies in the apparent madness of the latest development in consumer-credit proliferations—the entry of banks into a rapidly expanding, loan-plus-credit-card operation. The bait for this complicated hook of credit is merchandise, but in these new schemes it is the banker who turns retailer, at least so far as billing goes, and who thereby establishes contact with debtors somewhat in the fashion of the old-time flipper."

Flipping was once a disreputable term applied to the activities of certain credit gougers. Under such an arrangement a consumer who bought merchandise from a dealer would make his payments to a sales-finance company which owned the installment contract. In turn the sales-finance company either operated or had an arrangement with a small-loan office. If the consumer found himself overwhelmed in debt, he would be turned over to the small-loan representative who would sell him a second loan to cover all his payments. The second loan, of course, would call for much higher interest payments.

Today flipping has become respectable, though it is worked in a more sophisticated fashion under the euphemistic name of debt consolidation. The consumer who finds himself overloaded on a bank charge account may be steered to the bank's personal loan department where his debts are conveniently consolidated.

Although most consumers are unaware of the costs of bank charge-account plans, a number of merchants find the 6 per cent commission a stiff sum to pay. However, these merchants often have little choice in the matter, since they usually are small business men who must compete with the big credit operations of the large department stores. Perhaps a San Francisco merchant summed it all up when he explained: "Nobody claims to like the damn things but Giannini (of the Bank of America) and the women. We could fight the bank, but the women are going to make the cards a habit. They'd rather argue with the old man after charging a purchase than try to get money from him in advance."

The dealer's opinion, recorded by *Electrical Merchandising,* was offered during a conversation at a bar. The merchant had been shaking dice for the drinks. He lost, and paid with his Diners' card.

Of all the revolving credit schemes so far devised, none matches the bank plan that not only eliminates cash but allows the consumer to do his debt buying in any store in any city in the country. Variously called Check Credit, Ready Credit, Borrow-by-Check, and *Instant Money,* this ultimate gimmick in debt merchandising has blanketed the banking world like a snowfall of money. Its virtues are so simple and so enticing that by December, 1959, four years after it was offered by the First National Bank of Boston, over 182 banks across the nation had some form of *Instant Money*. With it consumers have bought bobbie pins, bottles, dinners, flowers, bassinets, boats and Thunderbirds. As Harold B. Hassinger, a vice president of First National of Boston, told a meeting of fellow bankers: "We are still taking it slow, but don't be surprised if this plan ultimately displaces most everything but the open charge account—with the grocer, the druggist, the gas station, and the other types of retail outlets, where a charge account is justified more for convenience than for credit purposes." It appears that *Instant Money* is bringing in immediate profits at a rate that even amazes the most experienced debt merchants.

A typical plan works like this. The consumer is permitted to make out checks without depositing any money in the bank to back them up. By writing an *Instant Money* check, often distinguished from regular bank checks only by a different color, the customer has in effect taken out a loan from the bank which he will repay in monthly installments. The check can be used anywhere a personal check would be accepted, although trivial expenditures are discouraged. Like most revolving credit, as each payment reduces the loan, it simultaneously increases the available credit from which the customer can draw. Although costs to the consumer vary, they can be fairly high. They usually run 1 per cent a month or 12 per cent true annual interest on the unpaid balance, a .6 per cent charge for credit life insurance which the borrower pays but which protects the lender in case the borrower dies, and a fee of 25 cents for each check used. By the spring of 1959, First National of Boston was able to announce that it had over seventeen thousand check credit accounts on its books. By the end of the same year the American Bankers Association reported that in a survey of 465 banks, 182 had some form of bank check credit. The credit extended under the bank check plans at that time totaled nearly $200 million. For the banks the profits appear fantastic. First National announced that its net profit on Check Credit in 1958 was 92 per cent higher than on personal loans.

One of the paradoxes of bank check credit is that it is virtually proving too popular with the public. Continental Illinois National Bank & Trust Co., in Chicago, recently spent eighty thousand dollars on a campaign advertising its check credit plan. At first the campaign seemed amazingly successful, because eleven thousand people applied. The bank, though, received an understandable shock when it found it had to reject six thousand or more than half of the applications as poor check credit risks. As one New York banker put the problem: "Some people got the mistaken notion from the ads that banks were giving money away."

Many banks, however, are even earning profits from the people they reject. If the applicant is not good enough for check credit, he may be shifted to the more rigidly controlled small-loan department. Check credit is bringing customers into the bank that once were lost to the small-loan companies. As a form of sheep-shearing it is hard to beat.

Besides the small-loan companies, a number of merchants have complained that bank check credit subverts the loyalty of their customers. The consumer, with all that *Instant Money* in his wallet, can go any place he pleases. Most bankers simply shrug at such criticism. Some even insist that the merchants are rumbling out of the wrong side of their cash registers. Check credit, they say, does not compete with the retailer. The consumer uses it when he has no more cash or when he has extended to the limit the credit the retailer will allow him.

The Citizens & Southern National Bank of Atlanta, Georgia, is one institution that put its money where its experience lies. C. & S. offers both a bank charge-account plan and bank check credit. Leo L. Rainey Jr., assistant vice president, explained it this way: "We do not feel that there is necessarily any relationship between *Instant Money* [C. & S.'s check-credit plan] and merchant purchases, for we are convinced that we have found an entirely new market for lending funds in our bank. We are finding more and more that the bulk of our *Instant Money* business comes to us from the loan sharks [victims], the salary buyers, and from [people who use] other banks. We are convinced that they look upon this as a painless method of stretching their budget during the painful times and that to them it is an easy, convenient, dignified way to pick up the cash necessary to enjoy the flexibility in their budget which they must have in order to live a satisfying life."

A similar but more candid opinion was expressed by Harold B. Hassinger, vice president of Boston's First National. "Just for a moment," he said, "let us consider the financial problem of the average family man. He has to meet an annual round of expense peaks that are hardly ever geared to his weekly or monthly income, although they may in the aggregate be well within his annual income. He may be faced with quarterly or annual income tax payments, periodic life and fire and other insurance premiums, vacation expenses, house repairs, fuel bills, and clothing and furniture expenditures, not to mention medical and other emergency types of expenses. Any of these can peak up and be a problem in a given month or a given two weeks pay period. First Check Credit is the one best answer to this problem for it enables the man to meet his peak obligations in cash as they arise and to pay off in a sensible series of even monthly payments geared to his income."

Peaking-up is simply another way of saying that no matter how the Ralph and Alice Homers plan their budget, their debts will get the better of them. However, if they are still credit-worthy, they can turn to bank check credit. A blessing of check credit is that the Homers, once they find themselves overloaded, can "unpeak" with a do-it-yourself form of debt consolidation.

On occasion a devotee of bank check credit not only con- solidates his debts but may quadruple his obligations. *Home Furnishings Daily* records the case of a man who owed $800. The debtor had been given a $900 line of bank check credit. He used $300 to pay up three delinquencies on another bank loan. The remaining $600 was spent on the down payment for a new car. Instead of owing the original $800, he was $3,000 in debt. It appears that revolving credit has given some consumers a new horizon: debtor's peak or bust.

The danger inherent in this new concept of credit is sub- tle, but alarming. The essential perversion is that the sale of credit itself has become the ultimate purpose. The result is a form of economic immorality, whereby the consumer, who is being sold debt, receives something which has no func- tion. To put it another way, the distribution of goods and services, once a prime purpose of credit, is no longer the main function of many merchants and manufacturers. Profit derived from the finance charges has become the main end.

There is the additional, inescapable fact that the consumer is frequently incapable of calculating the cost of the finance charges he pays. These costs are not only hidden but it appears that a concerted effort is being made to insure that the consumer remains a credit ignoramus. Thus the consumer pays for debt, something from which he may receive no benefit, at a cost of which he is ignorant. The result is that the debt merchant makes a profit through deception. There is little question that the consumer is being taken, even by the most respectable business institutions in the country. Indeed, the measure of this deception is not where it exists but its degree. The extent to which some debt merchants have turned deception into plunder, and the tragedy that has resulted, will be described in the next chapter.

9 Caveat Emptor: Chant of the Credit Gougers

> We started selling this refrigerator for $250. The customer would make a $50 down payment. Then as soon as the weekly payments fell behind we would repossess it. We would then lop $25 off the total price and sell it again. We must have sold and repossessed this same refrigerator over a half-dozen times. The last time we carted it out of somebody's house it even had food in it.
>
> *A former employee of a high pressure appliance store recounting his experiences.*

It was another winter's day in Chicago. Rain and snow enveloped the city in a raw chill and darkness hung in the sky. For William Rodriguez and his family, this day—Friday, February 5, 1960—was the prelude to terror and tragedy.

The day began with a medical examination. Since Monday, William had been recuperating from the flu at his apartment on Chicago's West Side. The apartment with its five rooms in need of paint and its linoleum-covered floors was home to William, his tiny, dark-haired, dark-eyed wife, Nilda, and their four children, the oldest seven, the youngest one month. There were times when William Rodriguez wished the rent was a little more manageable. Out of his take home pay of $240 a month, he had to give the landlord $87.50. But on that Friday, February's unpaid rent was a small thing that pressed upon him. Ironically, the only warm ray for William Rodriguez was his health. The doctor at the medical examination told him he had recovered from the flu and that he should report Monday to his job as a mail-order clerk for Sears Roebuck.

William Rodriguez did not return home from the medical examination. For the next twelve hours, perhaps longer, he wandered from movie house to darkened movie house, his mind desperately seeking the illusions of the great silver screen. Finally, the projectors were still and William again walked the now almost silent streets. Before returning to Nilda and the children, he stopped at a drugstore where he purchased a substance used to destroy rats. Slowly he trudged through the rain and snow, eating the poison.

At 2 A.M. he arrived at his apartment where Nilda was waiting for him. William, his body already in convulsions, told her what he had done. Nilda called the police and they took him to Bethany Hospital where he was given fluids and his stomach was pumped. Nilda wanted her husband to remain at the hospital, but the doctors said it wasn't necessary for him to stay and that she should take him home. She lacked cab fare. But a neighbor who had gone to Bethany drove them back to their apartment. Mrs. Rodriguez had been told that if her husband became worse, she should call Cook County Hospital. So when the sickness returned a few hours later, Nilda again called the police. As they drove to the hospital, Nilda called out, "William, William." But her husband did not answer her. He was pronounced dead on arrival at Bethany, the same hospital that had previously sent him home. As the police carried him into the street, a letter dropped from his pocket. The letter had been sent by a Chicago firm that had sold William a second-hand television set on time for $200. The set had broken down the day after he had received it. The firm threatened to stop his pay unless he brought in $45 of the $172 he still owed. William received the bill on Thursday. He had until Saturday, the day he died, to make payment.

William Rodriguez was to live in death as he hadn't in life. His name and story were to appear in all the Chicago newspapers and two intrepid Associated Press reporters, Earl Aykroid and William Conway, were to record the travail of the twenty-three-year-old Puerto Rican, their report traveling to papers throughout the land.

William Rodriguez, they learned, was a deeply devoted man; nothing was too good for his family. As one friend said, "He was happy-go-lucky and generous. He simply wouldn't listen to advice if it meant giving up something for Nilda and the children." William's second failing was summed up by another friend: "He would always take anybody's word for anything when buying things. He wouldn't read anything." For the debt merchant without a conscience William was the ideal customer.

William Rodriguez did most of his shopping in the Roosevelt Road area in Chicago's West Side where one word, "credit" shouts from nearly every window. It was there that William bought furniture, clothing and jewelry, all on time. On Mother's Day he gave his wife a religious medal which he bought on credit. The medal was later valued at 50 cents. William was charged $30. From a furniture store, he bought $528 in household goods. At the time of his death he owed the store $508. It was later testified the store had allowed William this much credit shortly after it had attached his wages for a $167 debt, which was paid.

It even reached the point where the debt merchants actually charged William for goods he never purchased. Once a stranger came to Nilda's door and left a bedspread. The stranger said it was for a neighbor and that he would pick it up the next day. He never came. Shortly thereafter William's pay was garnisheed for $34.

At the time of his death, he owed about $700 in all. Although his wages had been stopped three times previously, there was no judgment against him when he died. This time, though, he feared new garnishments might mean the loss of his job. And he knew, too, that even if he wasn't fired, the garnishments would cause endless hardship on his family. He would be forced to give his creditors one-quarter of his $60 a week take-home pay. In addition, half his month's wages would have gone for rent alone. All he would have had left was a little over $20 a week to feed, clothe and care for Nilda and the four children.

On March 23, the coroner's jury returned its verdict: "Suicide while temporarily insane due to pressure from creditors." One may question whether William's act was the result of temporary madness. For when he died he left a $7,000 insurance policy that he had taken out with Sears, his employer. In terms of the society that permits the sucking greed of the credit gouger, William Rodriguez, the good provider, knew that for his family's existence his worth was infinitely greater in death than in life.

The tragedy of the Rodriguez family is unusual but not unique. Arthur K. Young, director of the Legal Aid Bureau of United Charities, told the Douglas Committee he knew of a second debtor's suicide and possibly a third in Chicago since 1957. Not uncommon, however, are the depredations practiced by the credit gougers. Their victims almost invariably are people with low incomes, usually unsophisticated, and frequently those whose need for credit is greatest. The gougers' potential prey, usually those who earn less than $4,000 a year, is legion. There were 23,400,000 consumer spending units* in the United States whose income did not total $4,000 in 1959. Unfortunately, with all the myriad statistics gathered by federal, state and private organizations, no attempt has been made to estimate how many people are victimized yearly by the credit crook. A conservative estimate, however, must number in the hundreds of thousands. Consider just the amount of goods sold on time by door-to-door salesmen, frequently the most avaricious credit gougers. At a trade show held recently in New York, it was estimated that house-to-house salesmen annually sell one billion dollars worth of merchandise on credit. Further, it is not unusual for a door-to-door salesman to charge as much as 300 per cent interest. And this type of credit thievery is only one of many. Perhaps even more impressive was the evidence presented before such groups as the Douglas Committee of the U. S. Senate and the Unruh Committee of the California Assembly. These federal and state committees heard hundreds of cases of credit abuses perpetrated against those who could least afford to be gouged. Finally, testimony before such committees stressed that although most businessmen are generally honest, no community exists that does not have its nest of credit vultures.

But more telling than statistics is the human tragedy that so often lies behind them. It is the life of quiet desperation, the ceaseless tension, the fear of ultimate impoverishment that haunt so many, who because of modest means find themselves chained to the treadmill of never-ending debt. One witness, L. S. Buckmaster, president of an AFL-CIO union,

---

* A spending unit is defined as all related persons living together who pool their incomes. Husband, wife and children under eighteen living at home are always considered to be members of the same spending unit.

recorded for the Douglas Committee the plight of the low income American family in this land of abundance.

I am going to quote a letter from a San Diego, California,
housewife. She described her family budget on an income of
$300 a month. You will see this is a conservative living family.
There are no liquor expenditures, no money for baby sitters,
for this couple cannot afford to go out. The budget is a tight
one with television as the only real luxury. I feel it important
to give a picture of an American working-class family because
workers are the people who most frequently come into contact
with "easy cash" finance companies.

This San Diego housewife writes: "I wonder sometimes how
people in our position ever get out of a hole?" Mortgage payments were $64.50. The family paid $60 a month on a $2,000
loan and made installment payments of $35 a month. That
was on some other items besides the main loan. Food for this
family was a monthly average of $125; utilities were $15; trans-
portation $25; insurance $14 . . . The outgo of this family
($338.50 per month) adds up to more than the income ($300).
At least the obligations amounted to more than the income.
This explains the note of restrained despair in the letter. It also
helps explain the reason so many modern, low-income families
are continually in debt to finance companies. Borrowing is
not a luxury to this family and multitudes of other families in
similar circumstances. Borrowing is necessary just to hang on.
Families in such circumstances will probably be dealing with
loan companies the rest of their natural lives, and they need
every possible protection the Government can give them. Every
cent and dollar they save becomes a vital one to their well-
being and happiness.

The credit crooks entwine themselves around just such families as described in Buckmaster's testimony. Yet it is these

families which can least afford the sums the credit gouger exacts. What is equally reprehensible is that the debt industry, through its own logic, sanctions the exorbitant rates wrested by the credit gougers from low-income families. It is an axiom that the rates for credit go up as earnings decrease, that the poor consumer must pay the highest finance charges for the privilege of buying on time. The debt merchants logically insist that they must charge more because low income debtors prove greater risks. Yet it is the low income families who, least able to afford debt, are frequently overloaded by the debt merchants themselves.

A typical community where credit chiselers operate is East Harlem in New York's upper Manhattan. It is a community of vast slums, of smells that shock the senses, of humanity packed and quartered like grains of wheat in rotted bins. Over four thousand people are housed in one block alone. And it is in this block between the decaying buildings where one finds an open dirt lot. The lot is not a playground but a debtors' graveyard. For it is there that the people of the block pile up the cheap refrigerators, the shoddy TV sets, the broken furniture that they bought on time. It is not uncommon for the people in the neighborhood to continue to pay for merchandise they have thrown away. During the Christmas and Easter seasons, when the lot brims with discarded merchandise, the New York City Department of Sanitation sends around a truck to remove the junk and clear the ground.

One resident recalled the memory he had of the door-to-door salesman when he moved into the block ten years ago. It was a dollar down, a dollar a week. The item usually was paid for within the first ten weeks. The remaining fifteen payments were the credit gouger's gravy. Ten years have passed, he said, but little has changed. The payments are the same and the goods are just as shoddy. The only difference is in the appearance of the time peddler. Once thin, unshaven, he made his rounds in clothes that were near tatters. Now, a decade later, he has grown a paunch and makes his weekly collections in the latest model car. The debt peddler, and there are thousands of them, is one of the questionable benefits of the consumer-credit explosion rarely mentioned.

The omnipresent influence of the credit gouger in East Harlem was vividly stated by William Kirk of the Union Settlement Association. Since the War, five low-income housing projects have been erected in the area. William Kirk's statement before the Douglas Committee refers to what has happened to the families, who, escaping from the surrounding slums, cannot flee the padding step of the credit chiseler.

"For the most part," he said, "our new neighbors are young parents; most of them have recently come to New York City either from the South or from Puerto Rico. They are not too familiar with the city and its ways. They come to these new apartments with high expectations. It is understandable how, on leaving the miserable quarters in which they have been existing, they want to achieve a better way of life—a comfortable bedroom, a TV set, furniture for their living-dining room. And of course there is the continued problem of clothing. Our neighbors have pressing needs— high expectations—and a strong tendency to believe what they see and hear on TV, or what salesmen tell them.

"Our neighbors are subjected to a consistent barrage urging them to buy, buy, buy—to buy now and pay later. This comes into their homes through TV programs—the aggressive selling program of many stores. The peddlers who are omnipresent will sell anything and will often go to amazing lengths to do just that. They are persistent, and their ingenuity is amazing. It is hard to describe the combination of pressures focused on our neighbors. More often than not, the items are shoddy, the cost excessive, and the terms vague."

The amazing ingenuity of the door-to-door credit gougers was described by Helen Hall, one of the nation's most respected social workers and director of the Henry Street Settlement on New York's lower East Side. Here is only part of Miss Hall's disturbing testimony:

Mrs. Brown let a man into her apartment who gave the impression he was from the housing authority. She thought he was a maintenance man or plumber. He walked in and installed a covering or panel underneath the sink in her kitchen. It improved the kitchen, and she thanked him.

"One dollar," he said.

"I thought the project sent you," she said with surprise.

"Oh no," he replied. "It's for sale. Everybody's buying. You agree the kitchen looks better."

She agreed and thought that for only a dollar it was certainly worth having a nicer kitchen.

But the salesman didn't go when she gave him the dollar. He then told her he meant that it was a dollar down and a dollar a week. Surely she didn't think you could buy all that for a dollar! It would cost $29. When she ordered him to take it out he insisted that all of the other neighbors had bought it and she wouldn't want her kitchen to be less attractive than theirs. Mrs. Brown gave in. Later she learned that the same sink panel could be bought at a department store for about $12.

When Mrs. Parker moved into the project she had the first bathroom which she didn't have to share with other families. Also her first shower. Hardly had she been in her new home when a peddler appeared at the door with a selection of bright-colored shower curtains. He showed her how she could save from her food money to pay a dollar a week for twenty weeks. Later, Mrs. Parker saw the same kind of shower curtains at a large store priced from two to four dollars. The curtain lasted a year.

High credit charges are not the only way the family pays. They pay in high cost and inferior goods. One woman bought a steam iron from a peddler for $20, which she says does not work as well as a make that sells for $8 cash. And she spent $30 for a bedspread from him, on time, which a friend saw in a store for $7.

Our interviewers found that ignorance of how much they were paying for credit came about largely because these women thought only in terms of the size of each payment and could not possibly have figured out interest charges or even total costs. But aside from those dealing with peddlers, none of the families interviewed actually knew how much more they were paying for credit buying. Those families who had received contracts for furniture had not understood them. In many cases there were no contracts at all, just a simple receipt or credit book. Where interest was noted it was often figured on the whole amount without deducting the down payment. Always it was an innocent figure such as 10 or 15 per cent. Usually there were a number of additional unexplained charges.

Implicit in the evidence presented by Helen Hall and William Kirk is that the credit gouger circumvents with surprising ease one of the stiffest and most far-reaching protective consumer laws in the nation. In 1957, the New York State Legislature, with the aid of Dr. Persia Campbell, then State Consumer Counsel, passed the "all goods bill." Among other protective measures it placed a limit on credit service charges

and required the seller to give the buyer a copy of the installment contract. This law has become a model for consumer
groups throughout the country. Yet the time peddler gets
around it by making his sale without any contract. If he
should be questioned, he can simply say the weekly payments
were all part of the cash price. Although the peddler himself has little or no legal recourse without a contract, payments are met because the sums are small and the customer
knows that if he reneges he will no longer be able to buy
from the door-to-door salesman, the best source for so-called
"easy credit."

The testimony offered by Miss Hall and William Kirk is
based in large part on the preliminary findings of a study being made on the consumer and credit practices in four New
York City low-income housing projects. The study is being
carried out by the Bureau of Applied Social Research of Columbia University. The investigators discovered that door-
to-door peddlers are but one thread in the credit knot.
Among other things they found elaborate funeral services being sold on the installment plan. Hundreds of airplane tickets to and from Puerto Rico were bought weekly on time.
About one-half of the families moving into the low-income
public housing projects obtained most of their furniture directly from high pressure furniture stores. They paid for almost all of it by going into debt. Interestingly, these low-
income families found themselves in the same predicament as
the young couples making their first move to suburbia. Both
groups were forced to buy on time so they could furnish
their new and larger quarters. The difference, of course, is
that the low-income families paid more for cheaper and
often shoddy merchandise. Just how shoddy was noted when

the researchers found the housing maintenance department sent a large truck around the grounds of one project three times a week to cart away defective and cheaply constructed furniture.

Typically, despite the persistent and sometimes tragic use of debt, it appeared that few if any of the families had any real concept of its costs. Helen Hall noted that in a survey of thirty-four families who had bought on credit, all but two seemed to realize that they had to pay for the privilege of buying on time. However, they had no idea of how much. Twenty-seven families were asked what they thought the true annual interest was. Not one, according to Miss Hall, seemed to understand what this term meant. When it was explained, twenty-three said they did not know what they were paying.

The families were then asked to list the price they paid for items bought on credit and to estimate the cash price of each item. According to their own estimates, most of the families knew that they were paying 30 per cent more for their furniture *aside from the cost of credit* than they would have if they had been able to pay cash. Four families gave figures amounting to more than 60 per cent and three claimed they had paid 100 per cent over the cash price. These families knew they were being taken, but there was little they could do about it.

The final question posed: what would you be willing to pay for a hundred dollar item on credit. Six families replied they would not pay more than 10 per cent of the cash price, or $10. Only four of the twenty-one families answering this question were willing to pay more than 20 per cent and none had any real understanding of what they had paid for credit. The investigators had discovered, as others before them, that in the wonderland of credit the poor and the well-to-do are deceived with equal impunity.

One of the more gruesome aspects of low-income debt is the weapon it offers unscrupulous employers who do not sell credit but who use it to blackmail their workers. The employers hire recent migrants, usually Puerto Ricans, at sub-standard wages. To keep the wages at an inhuman minimum, the bosses play on the dreams and hopes of the unsophisticated and poor. Dan Wakefield, in his stirring book, *Island in the City* (Houghton Mifflin Co. 1959) a report on Spanish Harlem, discovered just how this was done.

"The boss," he wrote, "also has his own devices for insuring the quiet and uncomplaining work of the other women. Since most of the people who work in such shops have little cash on hand at any time, they furnish their homes and families' needs with installment buying. A credit reference is usually needed, and the boss of the sweatshop is only too glad to provide it. He may even loan the women five or ten dollars to help them make the first payment. Then, when the time finally comes, as it did on 125th Street, that a union starts to picket and try to recruit, the boss tells the women that if they join the union or leave the shop he will call the furniture store or the clothing store where he has given his name as a reference and have everything that the woman is paying installments on taken away from her. This often means the entire furnishings of a home. The women are seldom anxious to test the challenge."

The ultimate terror is the never ending feeling of desperation that grips the families who are unable to meet their weekly and monthly payments. The Columbia investigators discovered in their preliminary survey that one-third of the families in one low-income housing project are delinquent rent payers. When the researchers asked why, they found that many use their rent money to put off a persistent bill collector. The result is a bind that mercilessly presses on the debtors and their families. They face eviction from their homes if they forego paying their rent in order to pay their weekly or monthly installments. If they pay the rent but miss the time payments, at the very least they will be assessed unreasonable penalties for lateness. Further, there is the threat their furniture and other household articles will be repossessed. Finally, if the payments are consistently late or in default, their wages will be garnisheed. And, as noted previously, it is not uncommon for employers to fire anyone whose wages have been attached. One may wonder when other civilized communities will pick up their morning newspapers to read the story of their own William Rodriguez.

Although the variety of schemes used by credit gougers would fill a how-to encyclopedia of commercial thievery, most of them hinge on a few simple gimmicks. Many of these fraudulent practices have been declared illegal by some states. However, the loopholes are often numerous and the shrewd credit gouger can switch from one to the other with impunity. Of course, a number of the schemes are still considered legal in some states and have been used with larcenous abandon. Here are the credit gougers' favorites:

The Blank Contract. One of the most nefarious, this device usually appears in one of two forms. The contract either contains a blank space between paragraphs or blank spaces within the written material of the contract itself. The salesman tells the customer to sign the contract and later fills in the blank spaces with whatever unconscionable terms he can get away with.

The following case, with its ironic and tragic consequences, concerned a contract that had three blanks, all of
which referred to the installment payments. The blank contract was signed by a sixty-seven-year-old World War I veteran
who owned a small frame house in Jacksonville, Florida.
Living with him were two children, his wife and a dependent
sister-in-law who required considerable medical attention.
The old gentleman had expected to retire. Under ordinary
circumstances he could have spent his remaining years in
peace and comfort since he qualified for his firm's and an old
soldier's pension plans. But such was not to happen.

The elderly gentleman had contracted with an itinerant
home-improvement company to put in a bathroom, some
screens and to do a little painting. The price agreed to was
$2,650. "At the time I signed the estimate and agreement,"
he wrote, "I was not informed that there would be an 8 per
cent interest charge on the unpaid balance which was to
be paid at the rate of $25.50 per month, nor was I advised
that 50 cents per month of the monthly payment was a bank
charge for collecting the amount for him [the contractor]. I
now find, after paying approximately $535.50 (twenty-one
payments at $25.50 each) that only $156.49 has been applied
against the principal balance, the remainder going for interest. At the present rate of monthly payments I am informed
it will take over seventeen years to amortize the balance."

The interest and carrying charges on $2,650, the price
originally agreed to, totaled an additional $2,832.50. Thus
the actual cost to build a bathroom, put up screens and paint
came to $5,482.50, more than the frame house was actually
worth. The elderly gentleman's one consolation is that he
probably will not live long enough to pay off the sum he

owes. This consolation, of course, is doubtful since the house itself could be repossessed after he dies.

This case was brought to the attention of the Douglas Committee by William A. Hussong, general manager of the Navy Federal Credit Union. Hussong noted there are 6,800 instances where the Federal Housing Administration has listed the names of dealers and individuals who are not eligible for FHA Title 1 financing. "For every one listed in this book," he went on, "there are probably twenty-five more that never are publicized. And all of them have the same recourse to this type of improvement financing. They handle it themselves. They handle it through gyp dealers. They handle it through small, usurious moneylenders. This is a very real problem."

You may wonder why anyone would be silly enough to sign a contract that has blanks. People should know better. The New York State Banking Department, which handles such cases, told me about a lawyer who bought a Lincoln car on time and signed a blank contract. He later complained that extra charges had been written into the contract. The New York State law specifically forbids the use of contracts that contain blank spaces. The lawyer knew the law, but he signed the contract anyway.

The lawyer's case is unusual. Most people do not possess his awareness. The credit gouger simply misleads the debtor by offering a rational sounding excuse. A credit manager for a retail store told an investigative committee just how this was done. It was the general practice, he said, in 95 per cent of the cases to get the customer to sign the contract in blank by saying: "We'll type it in later. My girl is busy at something else."

He also told the committee that to his knowledge the store's customers were never given copies of the contracts. It was the usual practice, he said, to tell the buyer that the cash price was the total price and later fill in the additional charges for insurance and financing. The collection manager had even seen customers' signatures being traced on documents by an employee in the office. He concluded by noting that the company was not interested in repossessing the merchandise because it was no good. What they wanted was the money and the finance payments.

Bait Advertising. This scheme has been given top priority not only by the credit gougers, but even by some of the more respectable debt merchants. This device consists of advertising an item at an extremely low price and then, when the customer goes to make his purchase, he is offered *inferior* merchandise at the bargain price or more expensive goods at a higher price. Although cash merchants were the first to employ bait advertising, it has become a common practice among debt merchants. Just make a check list of the week's ads that carry these come-ons: "No Money Down," "Low Bank Rates," "Our 6-Percent Plan," "Guaranteed Cash Reserve," "Name Your Own Terms." (And see how far you will get.) One of the most vicious schemes, the "No Money Down" plan, often means that people with low incomes end up signing two high-rate notes, one for the down payment and another for the balance. One "No Money Down 4-Per cent Plan" was found to be 4 per cent on the amount borrowed as a down payment and to be repaid in three months. Actually this came to 32 per cent a year in true annual interest on the down payment alone.

A typical case of the credit gouger at work and what can happen to his victims was illustrated in this story presented to an investigative committee. Not only was bait advertising used as a come-on, but these debt vultures actually used the law to help them in their swindle.

A family whom we will call Jones had seen a sensational offer on TV, a complete house full of furniture for $262. Mrs. Jones testified that when she visited the store she was only shown the more costly furniture. She added they induced her to buy the expensive set for $700 after she had been promised $400 for her old furniture. The contract was signed in blank. Nothing was said about a carrying charge. Not only did she not receive a copy of the contract, she testified, but the store informed Mrs. Jones that she now owed the store $840. In addition, no credit was given for the old articles she had traded in.

When the new furniture proved defective, Mrs. Jones sought an adjustment. But the store slammed its doors. In turn Mr. and Mrs. Jones refused to make payments. That was all the store needed. First the furniture was repossessed. Then the store slapped a deficiency judgment on the couple's paid-up car. The car was sold at a public auction. But the sale, the store claimed, did not bring in enough to meet the deficiency judgment, $70 in attorney's fees, and $5.45 in interest. Since the store had taken the couple's old furniture, the new furniture and their car, there was only one other item they could attach. The store's next step was to place a lien on the Jones' home. It was at this point Mrs. Jones sought help from the district attorney's office. The district attorney intervened and the store, in a moment of charity, agreed to drop the lien on the house and to return $400 to the couple. As the result of this attempt to refurnish their home through a credit gouger, the Jones family lost their old furniture, their new furniture, their car and, if it hadn't been for the district attorney, they would have lost their house.

Debt Pooling. This form of chicanery made its first major appearance in the early nineteen fifty's when the consumer-credit explosion was already roaring through the land. In theory, debt pooling or debt adjustment should perform a desirable social function.* A person experienced in debt management consolidates a harassed debtor's obligations and through a budget system enables him to adjust his financial affairs. Often the debt pooler is a swindler and a fraud. Without putting up any money himself or taking any risk, the debt pooler takes the debtor's money with the understanding that he will contact his creditors and work out an arrangement with them for paying his bills. For his services the debt pooler's fee may be 25 per cent of the debt plus an additional bookkeeping fee.

The following case involving a Philadelphia postal employee illustrates just how the debt pooler works. The postal worker sought out the aid of a debt pooling company which promised to relieve him of all his debt problems for a $500 fee. Since his debts were already $2,500 he now of course owed $3,000. The postal employee signed a contract under which he agreed to pay the debt pooler $50 every two weeks until the $3,000 had been crossed off the books. Six weeks later, after paying out $150, the postal worker had a caller, one of his creditors, who proceeded to repossess his car. Since no payments had been made the debtor attempted to cancel his agreement. The debt adjuster appeared most eager to oblige, providing he met just one debt, the $500 fee.

---

* Charles V. Neal Jr. is an interesting example of a scrupulous debt adjustor who has helped thousands through books, newspaper columns and his credit management offices in Des Moines, Iowa.

A short time later the postal worker discovered the debt pooler had not paid his other creditors, including a jeweler and a bank. At this point he sought the advice of the Legal Aid Society of Philadelphia who informed him that seventy others had complained about the company. The postal worker, like thousands of others, had just been taken by another credit gouger.

Probably the biggest debt pooler ever to operate in the United States was the Silver Shield System. In twenty months this company had built up a list of three thousand clients whose total debts exceeded four million dollars. Its offices were closed by Jacob K. Javits, then New York State Attorney General, shortly after the company had launched plans for nation-wide expansion through the sale of franchises. Javits noted later that Silver Shield had used about $70,000 in customer funds for its own purposes and not for the payment of clients' debts.

Since 1955, eleven states,* including New York and Pennsylvania, have outlawed or severely limited debt poolers. However, three other states—California, Illinois and Oregon —have passed legislation whose so-called regulatory provisions actually legalize the debt poolers' nefarious activities.

The Illinois debt poolers' law is an interesting example of the credit gouger's influence. As Richard B. Allen, counsel of the Illinois State Bar Association, put it: "By a remarkable legislative metamorphosis, H. B. 170, which was first an act that would have outlawed debt poolers, became an act giving them the trappings of legality through licensing and regulation." This metamorphosis occurred through the usual legislative maneuvers of amendments and wholesale substitu-

---

* The others are Florida, Georgia, Maine, Massachusetts, Ohio, Oklahoma, Virginia, West Virginia and Wyoming.

tions. The final irony came when the State House, which had originally enacted a measure to outlaw debt poolers by a vote of 127 to 12, reversed itself and voted without a dissenting vote to concur in the State Senate amendments which sanctioned the debt adjusters. Richard Allen noted that as a result of the Illinois General Assembly's actions the debt poolers "will be statutorily protected in charging some of the highest rates in the country and that their advertising will be spiced with the magic words 'state-licensed.' "

Under the Illinois law the debt pooler may charge as much as a 15 per cent fee of the total amount of the debtor's obligations. If the debtor drops out of the plan, he is required to pay 40 per cent of the total charge for the unexpired term of the program. In other words, the debt pooler receives two-fifths of the maximum fee for not settling debts. This provision is an invitation for the debt adjuster to discourage the debtor from carrying the plan through. Further, the law contains no limitation by which a plan would not be binding upon a debtor unless and until the debt pooler is able to get at least 75 per cent of the creditors to accept it.

It would appear improbable that in the mid-Twentieth Century a State Legislature would actually write a law that not only sanctions exploitation of debtors, but even defines the manner in which it would be carried out. Yet, unbelievable as it might seem, the Illinois General Assembly had done just that. But the Illinois guardians of the public trust are not the only ones to blame. There are thirty-nine states in the Union which have no law that prohibits the activities of the debt pooler. Thus, debt poolers are free to operate with legal immunity in four out of five states.

Wage Attachments. As described in Chapter 4, the respectable debt merchant may use garnishments to attach a debtor's wages when he reneges on the sums he owes. Even when used as a last resort by merchants with a conscience, wage attachment can mean misery and hardship. The credit gouger, however, will attach a debtor's wages not as a final recourse but simply to abuse, harass and swindle the low-income consumer.

George C. Chatterton, the Public Defender of the City of Los Angeles, told California's Unruh Committee: "Attachment of wages has been used in this State more as a weapon of vindictiveness than as a means of collection of debt. When a claim of exemption is filed by the debtor to secure the release of salary needed to support the debtor and his family and when the claim is allowed by the court, the debtor can look forward to further wage attachments by the collection agency or finance company. Before the debtor can secure a court order restraining further attachments, he has lost his job. Employers as a rule will not continue on the payroll an employee whose salary is attached more than twice. These continued wage garnishments can be for no other purpose than to harass the debtor because the creditor knows the claim of exemption will be granted by the courts."

The Los Angeles Public Defender went on to note that the wage attachment was abused daily, causing untold misery and hardship to hundreds. He added: "It always descends on low-income families that are totally dependent on a salary. In most cases, the earnings of the head of the family are barely enough to enable a poor existence."

Testimony before the Unruh Committee revealed that unscrupulous debt merchants would attach customers' wages when the merchants had failed to live up to the agreements they themselves had made. Some of the reasons wage earners were denied a living included the non-delivery of goods, merchandise that was not up to specifications and disputes over charges put into contracts after the debtor had signed them.

In its final report, the Unruh Committee noted that even though many debtors have justifiable defenses, they are ignorant of their rights under the law, and thus do not defend themselves. Further, they are unable to obtain the services of an attorney because lawyers "understandably shy away from taking cases when they are uncertain of the outcome and are not sure they will be able to collect their fees."

For some debtors, however, even the ability to hire an attorney to represent them actually results in an additional debtor's swindle. One of the basic principles of legal ethics is that no lawyer should represent both sides of a case. Yet in the wonderland of credit that is just what is happening. James Ganly, a representative of the Catholic Council on Working Life in Chicago, told the Douglas Committee that he has been running into this problem constantly for the last thirteen years.

"It is done in this fashion," he said: "An attorney may represent a loan company. Then, he has another office somewhere in the Loop, and people come in here to go bankrupt. So he takes the guy on for $300, and the guy is going bankrupt against the finance company that he is doing business with."

Ganly then went on to describe the typical case of the debtor whose defense attorney is also representing the creditor. The lawyer simply neglects to inform the bankrupt debtor that under the law he is required to return the automobile, coat or other goods he can no longer pay for. The result is a reaffirmation suit, which means the debtor owes for everything he went bankrupt on. This happens after the debtor has already paid the lawyer $300 for his advice.

Attempts to have these lawyers disbarred have failed because whenever they are caught they immediately settle the case. The lawyers know in most instances that the people they have just swindled live on a marginal income and are unable to take time off from work to fight their cases.

Perhaps the most telling description of the impoverished debtor's plight came from the pen of Milton S. Kronheim Jr., a judge in the Municipal Court for Washington, D. C. "The court," he wrote, "has them in every condition of poverty—wrapped in burlap, or blind, or a father cooking over a hot plate for five children while the mother is in a mental institution. This is no mere rhetoric, but a factual report greatly diminished . . . Recently a friend of mine who runs an automobile agency told me of having received a garnishment on one of his people who is paid $45 a week. The garnishment was for $974. When my friend asked the judgment creditor how a $45 a week man with a family could be given that much credit, the answer was, 'That's my business.'

"I submit that is an accurate answer—and it carried with it another question—Should the law court collect on his business?" *

The Hidden Finance Company. This venture in fraud is no different from a pickpocket plying his trade. Yet it is legal and is just another of the credit gouger's numerous tricks. In this instance the credit crook sets up a sales finance company that keeps the consumer in debt for worthless merchandise. The lawyers have another way of putting it. According to the law the defenses available against the original

---

* Due to the efforts of Judge Kronheim and the responsible members of the District of Columbia's business community, Congress passed a humane garnishment law in 1958 that has eased the impoverished debtors' plight.

payee are not available against the holder in due course of a negotiable instrument.

This legal folderol simply translated means that if you buy a piece of merchandise on an installment plan and the merchandise falls apart you still must pay the note which you signed at the time of the purchase and which has now been transferred to a sales finance company. The finance company may either be a separate company owned by the seller of the merchandise or it may have some working arrangement with him.

The hidden finance company is the favorite of the unscrupulous car dealer. Once the finance company brings suit upon the note, the buyer has no legal defense even though the brakes failed, the holes in the motor were plugged with wax and the engine fell out as he was rounding a turn.

The Parol Evidence Rule. This device simply allows the credit gouger's salesmen to promise the customer anything he cares to dream up and then legally break the promise. This gimmick is usually written into a conditional sales agreement with a statement that may read: "This contract constitutes the entire agreement between the parties and no verbal statement of any agent of the seller shall be binding unless incorporated herein." All this simply means is that the salesmen's oral promises have no legal effect once the contract is entered into. This clause has made meaningless many a credit gouger's verbal guarantees given shortly after the contracts were signed.

The Prepay Swindle. The last thing a credit gouger wants a debtor to do is to pay up his obligations before they are due. For the credit gouger this could mean a loss in finance and carrying charges. To discourage the man who wants to get out of debt, the credit gouger charges the debtor an exorbitant rate of interest, which the debtor must pay to regain his freedom.

A typical case concerns the man who was charged $125.70 interest to finance $378.75 for fifteen months. This comes to a simple annual interest of 50 per cent. After signing the contract, the debtor realized that this charge was exorbitant and tried to pay it off. After considerable argument and with the help of an attorney, the debtor was able to get the credit gouger to release him from his obligation. However, for the privilege of prepaying his debt, he had to pay $25 over the cash price. In terms of true annual interest this came to 130 per cent.* Prepayment charges, rarely mentioned in the contract, are levied with extraordinary frequency. It has been the unhappy fate of thousands of debtors to learn this fact of credit life; that once in the hands of the credit gougers the price of solvency and freedom is more costly than the bondage of debt.

The Balloon Note. A consumer tied to a balloon note by a credit gouger almost inevitably finds his debts have literally gone into orbit. This gimmick is being used increasingly among low-income buyers. The balloon note consists of a series of low monthly payments plus a huge final payment. Since the final payment is so large it invariably needs to be refinanced. The debt is never-ending.

This typical case occurred in Cleveland, Ohio. An elderly woman bought a car on which the time balance came to $2,543. Her debt was to be paid in eleven monthly payments of $50 plus a final payment of $1,993. She managed thirteen payments of $50 or $650 and then found she had to refi-

---

* The prepayment fee in terms of true annual interest is higher because the borrower had the use of the loan for a shorter period of time. For a more detailed explanation see Chapter 6.

nance. This meant that at the end of a year's time and after paying $650, she had reduced her debt by $26 or 1 per cent. At that rate it would have taken her roughly one hundred years before she could claim title to the car.

The degradation and hardship experienced by thousands of low-income debtors could easily be alleviated if all debt merchants and credit gougers sold credit that is reasonable. As Judge Kronheim put it: "If it is obviously unreasonable to credit a $35 domestic with a $476 television, and it *is* reasonable to sell her a $19 radio, then people who are in business should be able to tell where reasonableness begins and ends."

Unfortunately, Judge Kronheim's plea has gone unheeded. As the credit gougers descend into the market place, they cloak themselves in that ancient and devious slogan of the cheat: Caveat Emptor—Let the Buyer Beware. It means that the unconscionable seller of debt may abide by a special morality which places him above the rules of decency and honesty. For the credit gouger, though, there is only one all-pervading dictum: exorbitant profits no matter what the human cost.

10 *The Shark Has Pearly Teeth*

The gunman entered the small-loan office, pulled out a revolver, aimed it at the girl at the reception desk, and said, "Put the money in this paper bag." The girl looked at him with the coldest blue eyes you ever saw and snapped, "You can't have it. It's against company policy." There was only one thing the gunman could do. He turned and fled.

Related by the branch manager of one of 1,200 small-loan offices belonging to Beneficial Finance.

Ever since man recorded his first attempts at justice under law, his conscience has wrestled with the problem of *Debtors' Rights*. Over four thousand years ago the King of Babylonia caused to have chiseled the famous Code of Hammurabi on an eight-foot block of diorite. Under that ancient law, the first code to take up the plight of the borrower, there was to be no exploitation of the debtor by the powerful and rich.

By the time the Old Testament was written, the Code of Hammurabi as it applied to debtors' justice was already ancient history. In its magnificent prohibitions, the Bible commanded in Deuteronomy: "Thou shalt not lend upon usury to thy brother; usury of money, usury of victuals, usury of anything that is lent upon usury."* The problem of usury

* An historical inaccuracy, perpetuated to this day, is that in ancient Israel, the foreigner in need might be charged interest, but not the Israelite. Actually, no Jew could charge interest on loans made to the needy. Dr. M. R. Neifeld noted in his recent book *Neifeld's Manual of Consumer Credit* (Mack Publishing Co. 1961): "The Mosaic writings do not explicitly state that

was dealt with again in the Twelve Tables of Rome, the Justinian Code, the reforms of Solon and Caesar and in numerous papal bulls and encyclicals. Indeed, almost every philosopher, both secular and religious, has striven to define the debtors' rights and the interest the needy borrower should pay the lender. Yet a seemingly strange thing was to happen. The usury laws, which severely limited the interest that could be charged for borrowed money, were to be defended by those money lenders who in fact sought and received exorbitant rates of interest. Furthermore, those who worked to void the usury laws and raise the interest rates were the supporters of the poor, social workers, reformers and men of charity. How this has come to pass can be described in part through a review of the history of the consumer finance companies, who specialize in small loans, and their battle against the loan sharks or illegal lenders.

It would appear that on the subject of usury, where an exorbitant interest is exacted from the man who borrows money, the American conscience developed to an Old Testament edge. Forty-two states have passed laws that prohibit usurious charges.* Four additional states have set maximum general interest rates that range from 6 to 12 per cent a year. The purpose of these laws is to protect the debtor in time of need from being forced to pay outrageous sums for the

---

foreigners were charged interest as traders rather than as non-members of the Palestine community, but the genuine distinction between moneylending for consumption goods and for investment to earn more money, is inherent in the command that loans to relieve distress must be interest free for Gentile as well as for Jew. In Palestine of the Old Testament there was in fact clear distinction between relief measures and economic enterprise."

* Four states which have no usury laws are Colorado, Maine, Massachusetts and New Hampshire.

money he borrows. Yet these usury laws were responsible for the very practices they were supposed to prevent.

The explanation for this phenomenon can be found in the awakening of America from a rural economy to a highly industrialized, urban society. Twenty years before the Civil War only 11 per cent of the population lived in urban communities. By 1860, the figure had grown to 20 per cent; forty years later the figure had doubled again, reaching nearly 40 per cent. The movement to the cities meant this pioneer nation of farmers, hunters and ranchers was swiftly becoming a land of workers and laborers, men who could no longer count on the soil to sustain them during hard times. In case of an emergency such as a depression, illness or loss of employment, wage earners could only seek immediate relief through credit and charity which were pitifully insufficient if the need was widespread. The result was an ever growing demand by the new army of industrial workers for a place where they could borrow money to tide them over during difficult periods. This need, however, was met with an almost unprecedented outpouring of greed. The loan shark had surfaced on the national scene.

The extent of loan shark operations was summarized by Arthur H. Ham, one of the early battlers against a national scandal that in retrospect was to rival the evils perpetuated by Prohibition. In 1911, Ham was to note, ". . . every city in the United States of more than 25,000 population containing to any appreciable extent citizens dependent on fixed salaries or wages is infested with loan sharks in the proportion of one to five thousand and at least 20 per cent of the voting population are discounting two days' labor for the immediate price of one."

The loan sharks could attribute much of their success to the low interest rates fixed by the usury laws. It was not uncommon for these illegal lenders to charge between 60 and 500 per cent true annual interest on loans ranging from $5 to $300. The loan sharks had little to fear. The usury laws were seldom enforced and hence easy to evade. The penalties proved so mild as to be meaningless. But, most important of all, the laws were completely unworkable. The ethical lenders or consumer finance companies simply could not operate under the usury statutes without going bankrupt. The 6 to 12 per cent annual interest charges allowed by the usury laws were much too low to meet the costs of making small loans. Unfortunately, awareness and acceptance of this fact was so slow in coming that for more than a quarter of a century the loan sharks were virtually permitted to commit economic rape of a large proportion of the population of the United States. Like the Eighteenth Amendment to the Constitution, the state usury laws by forbidding "sin" created a national evil. As the Prohibition Era gave rise to organized crime, so the states' prohibitions against usury fostered organized loan sharkery.

No state better serves to illustrate the brazenness and cruelty of the loan sharks than Alabama, which until the fall of 1959 had extraordinary power. A haven for usurious operators, Alabama could claim the dubious distinction of supporting over two thousand loan sharks. In one county alone there were one hundred fifty illegal lenders, more than the total number of ethical small loan companies in the entire state of New York, the most populous in the nation. The results of this loan shark activity could be measured by this amazing fact: Alabama, which accounts for a little more than 1 per cent of the population of the United States, could claim more wage-earner bankruptcies than all the rest of America and its territories combined. Further, 70 per cent of those who had been driven into bankruptcy had debts with three or more loan sharks. In 1958, their annual take in illegal interest charges alone totaled an estimated eighteen million dollars.

For many low-income families in Alabama there was no other choice but to seek out the loan shark. One of the most reprehensible abuses consisted of loan sharks filing phony derogatory reports about their victims with legitimate credit bureaus, thus preventing people with moderate incomes from securing credit from other sources. Guy Sparks, executive assistant to the Alabama Commissioner of Revenue, and one of the state's vigorous crusaders against loan sharks, declared, "Such practices had dreadful consequences for the low-income family. It made them absolutely dependent upon the loan sharks whenever they needed money or credit for anything.

"As an interesting sideline," he added, "the most frequently given reason that low-income families began their dealings with loan sharks was to secure money for medical treatment. This medical treatment involved a doctor's bill, a drug bill or a hospital bill. Hospitals demanded a cash deposit to secure admittance. They convinced most low-income families that the patient could not leave the hospital until the bill was paid in full. Doctors became almost impossible for these families to get unless they were assured of payment. Drugs could not be secured by these families without payment. To get this money they turned to the loan sharks."

When an Alabama debtor didn't meet his payments on time, he was harassed beyond human endurance. The loan-shark collector frequently worked at night. He would phone a debtor every ten minutes, or call at 3 A.M. and threaten to remove the bed the borrower was sleeping in. If the loan-shark victim refused to open the door, the collection agent would stand in the yard and embarrass him by shouting loud enough for the neighbors to hear that the borrower refused to pay his debts. When these tactics didn't work, the loan sharks turned to violence. Debtors were beaten, shot, crippled for life. In one instance a young woman was so harassed by loan-shark collectors that she strangled her two-year-old son so she could collect a $1,000 insurance policy on the baby's life. She planned to use the money to pay off her tormentors. Her total debts came to $150. Another collector, operating at night, blindly fired into the home of a debtor after he had promised to make payment the next day. The bullet passed through the eye of the debtor's aunt, killing her almost instantly. Unbelievably, this reign of terror reached its height during the late nineteen-fifties.

Despite an increasingly troubled citizenry, the Alabama loan sharks continued to operate openly and with voracious abandon. They were able to do so for two reasons. The state usury law, which set the maximum interest rate at 8 per cent a year, was a crude mockery. The law, first written in 1818, a year before Alabama joined the Union, had been consistently amended in favor of the loan sharks. Then in 1945, the state legislature passed the Harris Act which contained this preposterous clause, "the charging of interest at a rate in excess of 8 per cent per annum shall not be deemed to be a criminal offense, but nothing contained in this chapter shall be construed as legalizing the charging of interest at a rate in excess of 8 per cent per annum." In other words, the Harris Act reaffirmed that the loan shark was breaking the law if he charged more than 8 per cent. Yet, in doing so, according to law, he had committed no crime. This fantastic loophole allowed the loan sharks to continue charging anywhere from between 250 to 2,000 per cent a year interest. At the same time the usury law, with its low maximum interest rates, kept the legitimate lender out of Alabama. For most wage earners who needed cash in an emergency, the loan shark remained their only recourse. In addition a number of state legislators were retained by loan sharks to represent them in court.

The loan shark and credit-life-insurance abuses became so reprehensible that the situation finally reached the United States Senate. In the fall of 1957, the Senate sent a subcommittee of the Judiciary Committee to Montgomery. Governor John Patterson, then attorney general of Alabama, testified: "They [the loan sharks] have a strong lobbying organization in the state consisting of over five hundred members. They are able to hire the best legal talent and they spend huge sums of money to beat down any attempts to correct the iniquities in the law."

Patterson's testimony was the result of the first all-out drive against loan sharks in the state's history. The origin of Patterson's battle was touched by an unusual drama. His father, Albert Patterson, was shot down by a gunman on the night of June 18, 1954, eighteen days after he had been nominated the state's attorney general. The elder Patterson had promised to end the fear and corruption that infested Phenix City, then a center of crime in Alabama. Albert Patterson's crusade included plans to clean up the community's loan sharks, many of them mere adjuncts to the local gambling casinos. The loan sharks would make loans to the victims of the gambling tables, many of whom were G.I.'s from nearby Fort Benning. The security the loan sharks demanded included tires, automobile accessories and clothing. Their interest rates, as usual, were exorbitant. Shortly after the elder Patterson's murder, John Patterson, then only thirty-one, was chosen to take his father's place. The battle against the loan sharks had begun in earnest.

John Patterson launched his first attack in the courts. His biggest stumbling block was the Harris Act, which held that usury was illegal, but not a crime. The young attorney general, however, had a trump to play, one that had been unwittingly dealt by some loan sharks. He ordered his staff to gather evidence on brutal collection methods and then went into court on a claim of public nuisance. He also insisted that even under the Harris Act the allowable fantastic interest charges also could be construed as a public nuisance. A test case finally reached the State Supreme Court in 1957 and Patterson's contentions were upheld. The victory, though it made headlines throughout the state, proved inconclusive. For it meant that the attorney general would have to proceed against each of the loan sharks, an endless process that might not be completed for decades to come.

The loan sharks, meanwhile, realized that though a battle had been lost, the war was far from over. They proceeded to employ another device whereby they cleverly hid the exorbitant usury charges. Called *bonanza packing,* it involved the tie-in sales of credit life, health and accident insurance at fantastic rates. Patterson, in his testimony before the Senate subcommittee, explained how this scheme worked:

". . . they were charging interest like this: they would charge $22 interest on a $30 loan for four months. In July of last year they set up and organized an insurance company. The five loan companies and the insurance company were owned principally by the same individual. Immediately after they set up the insurance company, they reduced their interest rates to 60 cents and then on a $30 loan thereafter they would charge 60 cents interest and $21.40 premium on life and health and accident insurance. They just used the credit insurance as a gimmick to get around the Alabama usury law."

Not only were the credit insurance premiums exactly the same as the previous usurious interest charges but the debtors in effect were paying these exorbitant sums for insurance that made the loan shark the sole beneficiary. During the initial six months the loan shark controlled insurance company received over $155,000 in premiums. Total claims came to $1,600 which, along with the premiums and commissions, ended up in the loan shark's pocket.

The only way Alabama could hope to end the loan shark terror was to pass a small-loan law which would set workable interest rates that would allow the legitimate lender to operate. An attempt to introduce such a law was made in the 1957 session of the state legislature. However, the law was bottled in committee and it never reached the floor. The situation reached a major climax in the 1958 gubernatorial campaign, when John Patterson, running on an anti-loan-shark ticket, was elected to Alabama's highest office.

The showdown came in the next meeting of the legislature when the State Senate underwent an exhausting thirty-five-hour filibuster. Up to the last moment, the loan-shark lobby actually planned their strategy on the floor of the Senate. Ironically the back of the filibuster, the South's sacrosanct parliamentary weapon, was broken by the second highest official, Alabama's Lieutenant Governor, Albert Boutwell, who suddenly and unexpectedly recognized an anti-loan-shark senator. The State Senate finally passed the bill on a 25 to 2 rollcall vote. It became law on January 5, 1960, exactly sixty days after it had been signed by Governor Patterson. Under the new law, legal lenders can charge 36 per cent interest a year on that portion of a loan balance of $200 or less and 24 per cent on that portion of a loan balance of between $200 and $300. However, on loans of $75 or less the interest rate is considerably higher, with the maximum rate of 240 per cent allowed on a $10 loan. The law also calls for violators to face six months in jail and a $500 fine.

Where the small-loan debtor is beginning to find a measure of justice in Alabama, the impoverished borrower has rarely been shown mercy in Texas, which at this writing still bears the unhappy appellation of "the Loan Shark State." The scourge in Texas has reached such huge proportions that it is doubtful that any state has supported as many credit swindlers or debtor victims. Until recently cursed by an unworkable usury provision in its constitution that limited interest rates to 10 per cent a year, Texas could make the dubious claim of maintaining a loan-shark industry with annual volume of about three hundred million dollars. In fact, the operation is so vast that the loan sharks for descriptive purposes must be divided into two groups. One group, the small small-loan companies, number between one thousand and fourteen-hundred. Their loans, which range between $5 and $100, bring in an estimated yearly volume of as much as $60 million. The interest rate usually starts at 220 per cent. Though the second group numbers only 275, their annual volume ranges as high as $250 million. They deal almost exclusively in secured loans of between $100 and $3,000. Their effective interest rate ranges from 35 to 80 per cent.

Typically, the most abused are those whose income is

lowest and who borrow almost invariably as a necessity. In Texas most of those who deal with the small small-loan shark are Negroes or people of Latin-American extraction. Their annual income generally is $2,400 or less. Besides having to pay exorbitant interest rates, these unsophisticated and needy borrowers frequently are the victims of debt pyramiding. A vicious scheme, it virtually enslaves the debtor who is unable to keep up with his payments. One case of debt pyramiding concerned a Houston borrower who started with three $50 loans from three separate loan companies. Four years later she had paid about $10,000 to thirty-nine different loan sharks. Not only had she been unable to pay off the original $150 debt, but the loan sharks insisted she still owed them an additional $2,884.

When Ted Hansen of the Houston Better Business Bureau was asked if such cases were unusual, he replied, "Not in the least," and added: "To find the loan shark victim, you have only to stop ten people on the street. At least two of them will be in debt to the loan sharks. Loan sharks are everywhere and they're incredibly bold. I heard of a shark who stood inside the state capitol and cashed state employees' paychecks for them so he could get his loan payments."

Hansen described the average loan shark victim in Texas as a family man, steadily employed, who has been in debt for three years to twelve loan sharks. "The borrowers are not all dumb," he declared. "The very people educating our children—our teachers—were among the victims almost across the board."

The viciousness of the Texas loan sharks' collection tactics even surpass the methods employed in Alabama. Not long ago the switchboard of a leading Houston hospital was jammed for two hours with calls from loan sharks harassing a hospital maintenance employee who owed them money. Another loan shark forced an airman to interrupt a training mission. The collection agent called the air field and in an excited voice said, "You've got to connect me with airman . . . His wife's been in a car wreck and she's dying." The pilot, reached by radio, made an emergency landing. Rushing to the waiting telephone, the airman pleaded, "My wife, how is she?" The voice on the telephone chuckled, "This isn't your wife. It's the . . . . Finance Company. You're a week late with your payment. When are you coming in, you dead beat?" One victim, driven to suicide by the loan shark's harassment, couldn't even find peace in death. Two days after the funeral, the loan sharks were on the phone bombarding the widow with demands that she pay what her late husband owed.

The battle against the Texas loan shark was begun by the state's attorney general, Will Wilson, who has filed over three hundred anti-usury injunction suits. Interestingly enough, more than half of these suits are being defended by eleven attorneys who are also members of the state legislature. To date, the most noticeable progress has been made in the field of *bonanza packing,* where Texas debtors paid out a munificent ninety-two million dollars in credit life, health and accident insurance premiums from 1951 through 1957. The loss ratio averaged a meager 14 per cent, which means the insurance companies and the loan sharks kept eighty million dollars. In 1958, as a result of the Texas insurance scandal, the State Board of Insurance Commissioners drastically lowered the rates and by the end of 1959 total yearly premiums had decreased to less than two million dollars.

The battle against the loan sharks in Texas is reaching a

climax. On November 8, 1960, Texans voted nearly three to one to amend the 10 per cent usury provision in the state constitution. The legal interest rate, however, will remain at 10 per cent until the State Legislature fixes a higher, workable rate.

Organized loan sharkery soon may be a fish out of water. Besides Texas, only Arkansas, where in 1956 the citizenry unbelievably refused to amend the state constitution and thus allow passage of a small-loan law, and the District of Columbia, which is run by Congress, have no anti-loan-shark legislation. In addition four other states—Tennessee, Georgia, North Carolina and South Carolina—have small-loan laws which are badly in need of repair. The remaining forty-four states have passed fairly strict yet workable laws. This does not mean, however, that credit bandits do not exist in the regulated states. In many large industrial communities the loan shark flourishes despite all attempts to outlaw him.

It is perhaps ironic that one of the enduring answers to the loan shark stems from a legacy left by a man who died over fifty years ago. When Russell Sage, one of America's most successful financiers, passed away in 1906 he left an estate of seventy million dollars. The next year his widow, a former schoolteacher, set up the foundation which bears his name. In the years to follow the Russell Sage Foundation distributed thirty million dollars in such varied areas of public endeavor as medical research, education and social welfare. Almost from its beginning in 1907 the Foundation became aware that no ethical lender could operate within the circumscribed interest rates set by the usury laws. It was also apparent that the loan sharks were virtually the sole commercial source of loans for wage-earning families. To help remedy this situation, the Foundation began drafting a model bill that would supersede the state usury statutes.

The bill in part grew out of the experience the Russell Sage Foundation had in helping five states pioneer comprehensive small-loan laws. By 1916, the Foundation was ready with its first draft. Calling for strict licensing and other regulatory features, the original model bill allowed interest rates of up to 3½ per cent a month or 42 per cent a year on the unpaid balance. Furthermore, $300 was the maximum amount that could be loaned under the rates set by the model law. There were to be a total of seven drafts, the last in 1942. The sixth draft, made in 1935, kept the 42 per cent maximum interest rate on balances of $100 and less, but provided for a 2½ per cent a month or 30 per cent true annual interest rate of any loan balance over $100. In the final draft the interest rates were lowered to 3 and 2 per cent a month or 36 and 24 per cent true annual interest. The Foundation also suggested that the amount that could be lent in certain states could be raised to $400 or $500. To-day most states have limits which range between $500 and $1,500. California has set the limit at $5,000. By 1945, more than 90 per cent of the population was covered by small-loan laws. The Russell Sage Foundation considered its work about finished and withdrew from the small-loan field.

During those early years when the Foundation first became concerned with the plight of the wage earner, an imaginative young Virginia lawyer by the name of Arthur J. Morris was developing a plan to deal with the often desperate credit needs of low-income families. By the time he was thirty-five, this son of a North Carolina storekeeper financed the first car ever sold on time (1910) and organized the first credit life insurance company (1917). But the plan for which he is best known is the now legendary Morris

Plan, so named by a Georgia editor in 1912. The seeding for industrial banking took place in Morris' Norfolk, Virginia, law office shortly after the turn of the century. Some fifty years later, Arthur J. Morris, writing in *Personal Finance Law Quarterly Report,* described how the Morris Plan originated:

In 1906, there was hardly a Monday morning when I arrived at the office that I was not confronted with one or more individuals asking for my assistance in helping them obtain loans. I would invariably ask: "Why do you come to a law office?" Their reply would invariably be: "Because of your bank connections. We have been to every bank in the city, and no bank will make us a loan." In effect, the most uniform reply from a bank was: "We cannot make loans to individuals who are not in business and do not carry regular deposits with us."

I began to investigate several of these applicants and found them to have the human need for money. They held steady jobs with fair earning power and were persons of good character. Subsequently, I was able to persuade my bank clients to make some of these loans. Within a period of less than two years, several banks represented by my firm made loans totaling $40,000. I was compelled to guarantee each and every loan. My faith in humanity was well founded, as each and every loan was repaid.

These applications for loans continued to pour into our law office until they interfered with the daily routine of our law practice. My partners wanted to know if we were operating both a law office and a loan office. I, therefore, decided to equip an inexpensive office in a loft building over a wholesale shoe company, to which applicants could be referred. I employed twenty-two men and women and had them travel over the United States investigating conditions similar to those that were found to exist in Norfolk and other cities in Virginia. At the end of two years, the conclusion was reached that 80 per cent of the American people not engaged in successful business enterprises were hopelessly without access to credit.

On April 1, 1910, Morris started the Fidelity Savings and Trust Company of Norfolk with a capital investment of $20,000.* Under the Morris Plan the usury laws were to be by-passed. At the same time the interest rates, though greater than allowed by law, would not be exorbitant. The plan actually was divided into two transactions. The loan part of the transaction called for a lump sum payment when the total debt was due. During the life of the debt the borrower deposited small sums periodically in a savings account until a total equal to the amount of the loan had been accumulated. The total was then applied to the payment of the loan. Another way of doing it was to make periodic purchases of a so-called investment certificate which equaled the amount of the loan. When the debtor had paid in full for the investment certificate, the certificate would be surrendered for cash, which in turn would be used to pay off the loan. Both savings and deposits and investment certificates earned interest.

Dr. M. R. Neifeld in his book *Neifeld's Manual of Consumer Credit* gave this simple example to explain the plan. A man borrowed $60 under such a dual arrangement, repayable in twelve monthly payments of $5 each. Interest at 6 per cent was deducted in advance. Repayments were made in a savings account on which Morris paid interest at 1.5 per cent per annum to his borrowers. However, the true annual rate

---

* The first industrial bank was started in Newport News, Virginia, in 1901 by a Latvian immigrant, David Stein. Stein brought with him knowledge of such plans already in operation in Europe. However, under Morris the idea really took root.

of interest on the loan itself was 11¾ per cent. (Since an average of about half the sum borrowed is outstanding for the full period of the loan, the original interest charge of 6 per cent is nearly doubled.) Thus the legal or usury rate in the state fixed at 6 per cent was simultaneously adhered to and exceeded. As a result of this scheme Arthur J. Morris was on his way to fame and fortune.

In the next few years Morris received the backing of some of the most influential financiers in the nation. Among them was J. P. Morgan Sr. who endorsed the plan shortly before sailing for Italy, from where he was never to return alive. Years later Morris was to recall the encounter: "Mr. Davison told me to tell the 'big boss' why we were meeting. Since he said he was only able to be there for a few minutes, I endeavored to explain my program for the 'democratization of credit.' I shall never forget his response: 'Gentlemen, this young Southerner has a brilliant idea! Its beneficial potentialities to the people at large are beyond the imagination of any of us, and it should raise the standard of American living. However, its fundamental principle is not new to me. If you recall my testimony just recently before the Pujo Committee of the United States Senate in Washington, you will remember I made the statement, character is the basis of all credit.' "

Though the Morris Plan and other ventures were to make the young Southerner a rich man, Arthur Morris could have made an even greater fortune had he accepted a suggestion made by his Wall Street backers. As originator, Morris was offered a one dollar royalty fee on each loan. The young lawyer turned down the suggestion because he didn't want to damn the plan's future with a promoter's fee. Arthur Morris noted many years later that 170 Morris Plan banks with several hundred bank affiliations had loaned some ninety billion dollars. "My attention," he said wryly, "has been called to the fact that if I had accepted royalty, I would have collected many millions of dollars. While I do not regret the position that I took at that time, in the light of subsequent events I find that my hindsight is much better than my foresight was."

The social and economic revolution wrought by Arthur J. Morris and his industrial banking plan was to manifest itself in many ways. Not the least significant is the remarkable change that has taken place among the nation's twelve thousand commercial banks, until recently symbols of patrician stuffiness. Today the average banker seeks the wage-earning customer with all the verve of a girdle salesman during a fire sale.

This revolution in banking circles and the subsequent wooing of the consumer began May 4, 1928. For it was on that day that the National City Bank of New York, one of the world's largest financial institutions, opened its doors to the wage earner in need of money. Since then National City has extended nearly five billion dollars in personal loans, of which all but twelve million dollars has been repaid. To put it another way, only one-quarter of 1 per cent has been lost by the bank. Even during the Depression the percentage loss averaged less than one-half of 1 per cent. The wage-earning consumers, once considered by bankers as too risky, have proved better risks than banks themselves.

This discovery that the average man is a trusty fellow has permitted the banks to join the highly profitable consumer credit explosion. To attract customers to their personal loan departments, charge-it and *instant-money* plans, the banks have undergone a form of do-it-yourself plastic surgery.

Herbert Brean, writing in *Life* recently, described some aspects of the new look in consumer banking. "This new look," he wrote, "is most immediately evident in the architecture of the banks. Once they resembled ancient marble mausoleums but today they are glass-and-metal palaces. Inside, the old black and white of cold marble and harsh iron has been replaced by inviting boudoir pastels. Counters are lower and no longer barred, stacks of money are placed virtually within the customer's reach, and officers sit at approachable desks."

Brean goes on to note that these are only surface manifestations. Once put-in institutions, they have become takeout institutions. To attract borrowers, banks have been turned into community centers that more and more resemble settlement houses for the middle class. One New York City bank floods its lobby at Christmas time and offers an ice-skating show. A Phoenix, Arizona, bank gives teas, carillon concerts, and publishes a humorous newsletter. Still other banks have given free lessons to women in how to install a zipper and lay a tile floor. And in Cleveland the fashion-minded housewife can sign checks printed in four tweed-patterned colors to match her dresses.

Despite this mammoth effort to be folksy, the banks are still unable to match the strides made by the consumer finance companies or small-loan lenders. By July of 1960, the personal loans outstanding for commercial banks totaled 3⅓ billion dollars. At the end of the same period, the consumer finance companies, the legitimate lenders who specialize almost exclusively in small loans, had over four billion dollars outstanding. This fact in part is remarkable because the banks' rates, which may range between 12 and 18 per cent true annual interest, are considerably lower than the 24 to 36 per cent usually offered by the small-loan companies. Moreover, many of those who go to the consumer finance companies would be most welcome at the banks' personal loan departments if they would only apply. An explanation of why people prefer the "friendly" loan company was offered by an official in the consumer credit department of one of the largest banks in the country.

"The reason small-loan companies continue to grow," he said, "is that the banks in spite of everything they have tried to do, still appear morally superior in the public eye. With these marble walls and bronze fixtures we have created in ourselves a father image. Not so with the small-loan companies, with their friendly looking, second-floor offices. Never supercilious, their personnel are trained to be courteous and sympathetic without being condescending. You might say, when the public goes to a bank they frequently feel inferior. When they go to a small-loan company, they feel superior."

Though one may cavil with the banker's plunge into Freud, there is no question that the nation's large small-loan companies are benefiting handsomely from the consumer credit explosion. Indeed, their growth in the past ten years has been stupendous. In 1960, the two giants—Household Finance and Beneficial Finance—loaned three million borrowers in the United States and Canada more than a billion and a half dollars, a 200 per cent increase since 1950. The number of loan offices of the two chains rocketed from one thousand, ten years ago, to more than twenty-two hundred in 1960. These offices are located in nearly every state in the Union as well as every Canadian province. Beneficial even has a loan office in London and claims that a customer borrows money from one of its 1,200 branches every five seconds of every working day of the year.

Although the current burst in the small-loan business can be largely attributed to the increase in consumer debt, the early development of firms like Household and Beneficial sharply paralleled the growing influence of the Russell Sage Foundation and the passage of small-loan laws. Both firms worked closely with the Foundation. By allowing the consumer finance companies to operate profitably, it was hoped that they would provide the growing army of wage earners with the credit they so frequently needed on an honest, businesslike basis. It was also expected that the small-loan companies, by charging considerably less for their services, would drive the loan sharks out of business. This in essence was the small-loan companies' social and moral reason for being. The loan companies, of course, have a further aim in life, to make a profit. And they have been most successful. In 1959 alone, the combined net profits of Beneficial and Household came to forty-five million dollars.

Like any business, the money is made where the customers buy. With the big chains like Beneficial and Household, the business of making money is carried on in the branch offices. Although many branch offices loan as much as one million dollars or more a year, they invariably operate with only a few hundred dollars in the office till. At Household average daily loans per office in 1959 totaled $3,392. Yet cash in hand averaged only several hundred dollars. Household can function this way because during the same day's operation the branch offices took in an average of $3,196 in payments for loans previously made. This money, in turn, was immediately loaned to new borrowers. Thus, Household's money is constantly working in a continuous flow of loans and payments. Whenever there is a demand for additional cash, often precipitated by seasonal periods like Christmas or vacation time, each branch manager can immediately call on his office's local bank reserve, which averages over seven thousand dollars.

Another unusual aspect of the small-loan branch office is that the responsibility for its operation is left in the hands of exceptionally young people. A somewhat typical Household office that I visited was located in the heart of New York's busy garment and fur district. Edward J. Moshy, the head of the Household branch, was thirty-two years old and had been a branch manager for five years. He was not only responsible for the smooth functioning of thirteen other Household employees but was overseeing a volume of more than $1,250,000 in loans outstanding that had been made to nearly 4,500 borrowers, all of whom had to gain his final approval. In part, Moshy's rapid rise to executive responsibility is another reflection of the consumer credit boom and the small-loan industry's post-World War II need for experienced personnel.

Moshy's office, just one of forty-nine in New York City, is completely self-functioning. The branch manager and his staff are not only responsible for deciding who shall borrow and who shall do without, but also make all credit investigations, collections, adjustments for slow payers and even do their own skip tracing. This highly efficient machine, lubricated by over eighty years of Household know how, can, if need be, interview an applicant, have him fill out a fairly lengthy questionnaire, make a somewhat extensive credit check, and hand the borrower his cash, all within a half hour.

Much of the speed and efficiency of each office's operation can be attributed to a special phone system which allows the prospective borrower to feed to an operator all the credit information called for on a loan application. The application itself when filled out gives Moshy and his staff a complete portrait of the potential borrower, his and his family's income, holdings, and his current and past debt structure. In addition, each branch office can call on a small-loan clearing house. Known as the Lenders Clearing Service, Incorporated, these bureaus keep records of current outstanding loans. Supported and operated by the small-loan industry, there are approximately one hundred such agencies scattered throughout the country.

A major problem in any operation as vast as Household's is to decide just how strict its employees should be in lending the company's money. Thus, when the delinquency rate is on the increase, company policy calls for a tightening of its lending criteria. Conversely, when the delinquency rate drops, the criteria are liberalized. To make sure its policy is up to date, Household has Moshy and other branch managers dispatch daily a complete ledger of the day's business, including the amounts loaned, the sums repaid, and the credit life insurance charges collected. In turn this information, gathered from nearly eight hundred offices throughout the United States, is collated at a huge I.B.M. center run by Household in Chicago's Merchandise Mart. Within twenty-four hours after each day's close of business, the top executives of the company, located in Chicago's Prudential building, know to the penny not only how much its offices have loaned out throughout the country, but how much has been repaid and the sums that are delinquent.

Household's I.B.M. center serves other purposes besides

offering daily reports on the company's state of business. By compiling information on each borrower's marital status, his income available for loan repayments, use to which the loan is put, Household's economic and social analysts and statisticians know when to increase the maximum loan amounts allowed under the various state laws. Or if the maximum has already been reached, Household can seek changes in small-loan laws.

Out of this catacomb of statistics emerges this portrait of the typical Household borrower: Married, he usually earns between $3,600 and $7,000. (This is a substantial increase in income over his earnings of nearly twenty years ago when 88 per cent of Household's customers had annual incomes of $3,000 or less.) The average Household debtor now borrows over $450 at a clip, which is equivalent to a month's wages. The largest single reason he borrows is to consolidate overdue bills. Of the nearly two million loans made in 1959, over a half million were taken for this purpose. Another two hundred thousand-odd went to pay for travel and vacation expenses, while the loans made by another 320,000 borrowers were equally divided between automobile purchases and repairs and medical, dental and hospital bills. Even though Household's borrowers aren't quite meeting their loan payments the way they used to, still over 99 per cent of the outstanding loans are eventually paid up. This one per cent loss may seem small percentagewise. But it does mean that Household has to write off seven million dollars a year, a tidy sum out of any company's pocket.

To cut down the number of dead beats and delinquent debtors, several consumer finance companies have instituted credit scoring systems that attempt to eliminate the personal human factor in judging payment habits. American Investment Company of Illinois, which uses such a system, rates each loan applicant according to mathematical scores computed on the basis of the applicant's answers to questions about job status, income, home ownership and the like. These scores are weighed against the payment records of other borrowers who gave the same answers.

The growing practice of turning out mechanical debt merchants occasionally runs afoul of the debtor who simply defies classification. One case that almost created electronic havoc involved the woman who refused to meet her payments. Eventually she was taken to a mental hospital from where she regularly sent money to the loan company. But as soon as she was discharged and pronounced cured, her payments stopped.

Although most small-loan debtors do meet their obligations, some carry it to extremes. Perhaps no story better illustrates how credit worthiness has become a hallowed concept than the case of the schoolteacher who insisted upon paying her mother's debt. Each month the schoolteacher sent $10 to the small-loan company, even though she was not legally responsible for the loan. She explained that although her mother had died some time ago, she wanted to protect her mother's credit rating.

Consumer finance companies are constantly searching for new customers or getting old customers to borrow more. And like any business, they are not adverse to using the techniques of Madison Avenue. Many small-loan companies rely heavily on radio advertising, frequently scheduling their blurbs during commuting hours. One of the more effective campaigns is the so-called "Money Special" used by Beneficial during holidays and changes in the season. Nine parts puff and one part fact, the "Money Special" is a soft-sell frosting laid on a cake of freshly minted money. Here is a typical come-on:

> Once again, by popular demand, BENEFICIAL is offering its famous SUMMER MONEY SPECIAL as a convenience to its Preferred Customers.
>
> It includes cash to catch up on left-over bills—to get everything squared away at home . . . *plus* cash for vacation—for the trip you've always wanted to take . . . *plus* extra cash wherever you go—with your new 1960-61 BENEFICIAL International Credit Card.
>
> So, make your summer dreams come true—take advantage of BENEFICIAL'S *complete* SUMMER MONEY SPECIAL! To get the cash you need, just say the word—your money will be ready when you come by the office. Remember: "You're the boss" at BENEFICIAL.

After reading this ad, I wondered what the customer gained by borrowing during this special offering. Money is money, I reasoned. A hundred-dollar bill is worth exactly one hundred dollars. It can't be marked up or down. In fact, the only advantage that I would be interested in as a borrower would be a reduction in the interest rates. When I inquired, I was told there was no decrease in the interest rates.

Even though all small-loan companies eventually want to get paid, some actually encourage their borrowers to remain in a state of constant debt. One consumer finance company has a system in some of its offices called "building a fence" around the debtor. The purpose of this debt-selling scheme is to insure that the client does not look elsewhere for his loans. It works only in states where the number of maximum small loans made to each borrower is limited. In New Jersey, for example, the customer can take out only one $500 loan providing he does not have a car to secure a second loan. As soon as the borrower has made four or five payments and his balance is down to $300, the loan salesman calls the debtor and tries to sell him another $200. If the salesman succeeds, he has raised the debtor's loan to the $500 limit. This scheme has the added attraction of insuring the hooked debtor will not wander to the inviting greenery of another small-loan company.

"The key to our success," my informant went on, "and that of any loan company, is to increase our loans outstanding. As soon as the account is about to liquidate, we take immediate steps to renew the loan up to five hundred dollars, the maximum allowed in this state. One of the things we do is to find out if the customer has other debts. Then we call him up and offer to consolidate them. Our best customers, I might add, are the old-timers. At least we know their habits. The idea is quite simple. Prevent the customer from getting off the hook."

Although the small-loan companies expend great energy in increasing the number of debtors on their ledgers, one should not arrive at the misconception that they are giving money away. Despite the greater risks loan companies take compared to banks, small-loan lenders today still reject approximately 50 per cent of all new applicants. Except for credit unions, where the debtor has to be a member to borrow, hundreds of thousands of people look upon consumer finance companies as the only place they can obtain cash in an emergency.

The question I posed again and again: "Where can rejected applicants turn?" One small-loan manager summed it up when he said: "Some people we reject go to their family. Others do without. Still others must go to loan sharks."

How many? No one seemed to know. Once the small-loan customer is rejected, his case is dropped. Yet the number who become involved with loan sharks must be large indeed. In the fall of 1960, Frank Hogan, New York's District Attorney, reported netting two schools of loan sharks in Manhattan's garment district. Their annual take came to 2½ million dollars. The New York loan sharks were operating in one of the most strictly regulated states in the nation. In Michigan, another well-regulated state, the current annual profits for illegal lenders has been estimated as high as one million dollars. Outside the South, most loan sharks operate in the large industrial plants and on the city streets.

Despite the passage of small-loan regulations in almost every state and the growth of the consumer finance companies, there remains the inescapable conclusion that thousands of debtors still must turn to the loan shark, the most vicious credit gouger of all.

11 *The Peace of Mind Boom*

One credit life insurance company wrote a "peace of mind" policy for a member of the local constabulary who had a penchant for Russian roulette. During a demonstration he loaded the cylinder with one round, spun it and blew his brains out. The insurance company agreed to return the premium to his widow, claiming that "peace of mind" insurance did not cover "self-destruction."

A summary of testimony before the Langer Senate subcommittee hearing on credit life insurance practices in Alabama.

In the wonderland of credit anything can happen. It wasn't so long ago that our rustic, unsophisticated ancestors considered debt akin to a state of sin. Yet within the span of two generations being in debt has been turned into a virtue. Even more remarkable is the debt merchants' success in capitalizing on the uncertainty that afflicts us when we mortgage our future. For nearly every debtor fears that, should he die before his debts are paid, his family will be held responsible. Instead of proving a deterrent to debt, this concern not only helps creditors sell debt but has actually opened the way for one of the most lucrative forms of debt merchandising. This offering is called credit life insurance. The debt merchants have another name for it. They call it "peace of mind" insurance.

Each time a debtor borrows money or buys a car, furniture, or any other merchandise on credit, he may purchase a separate credit life insurance policy through the lender or merchant. The credit life policy will cover the debtor's obligation if he dies. For example, Ralph Homer originally owed a sales finance company $2,000 which he agreed to pay back in monthly installments. He also took out a credit life policy. Ralph managed to pay $600 to the company before he was killed in an auto accident. The $1,400 he still owed was paid to the finance company by the insurance company under the terms of Ralph's peace of mind or credit life policy. In effect, this means that although Ralph, a debtor, paid the premiums for the credit life policy, the chief beneficiary was the creditor to whom he was in debt and who also had served as the insurance agent.

The recent success of credit life is phenomenal. According to the Institute of Life Insurance, credit life in force in the United States as we entered 1961 covered more than one-half of all the outstanding consumer debt in the nation. By the beginning of 1961 over thirty billion dollars of this insurance was in force, a 1,000 per cent increase over the past decade and a 7,000 per cent increase since the end of World War II. At the end of 1960 there were approximately over forty-three million peace-of-mind insurance policies outstanding, a 2,000 per cent jump over the past ten years alone. Measured in another way, on a percentage basis the boom in credit life has even outstripped the consumer credit explosion.

The purpose of credit life is undoubtedly a worthy one. If the time buyer who has purchased peace-of-mind insurance dies, neither his widow nor his heirs will be troubled by his debts. It also means that the debt merchant is not only insured against loss but, equally important, he is not put in the embarrassing situation of having to collect from the deceased debtor's family. Since debt is merchandised as a convenience and not as a harrowing experience, the public re-

lations benefits in credit life for the time seller are ines-
timable.

Undoubtedly a major reason why peace-of-mind insurance
has enjoyed such a remarkable growth is that the nation's
debt merchants have discovered that selling credit life is a
highly profitable business. These profits are divided among
sales finance companies, small-loan companies, banks, auto
dealers, department stores as well as the insurance companies.

Once the market potential for peace-of-mind insurance
was realized, there was a decided rush to get into the business. Today there are at least fifty companies which specialize just in credit life. A second category consists of the
all-purpose insurance companies, including Aetna Life,
Equitable Life of New York, John Hancock and Connecticut General. Prudential, another all-purpose company, is
the biggest credit life insurer, accounting for more than
seven billion dollars or more than one quarter of the total
outstanding peace of mind insurance. The third and most
recent entry into the field are the major sales finance companies which have set up their own captive insurance companies. In 1953, Associates Investment Company, one of
the larger sales finance firms, set up Alinco, which serves
as a reinsurer of credit life policies. At the end of its first
year Alinco had a capital surplus of seven hundred thousand dollars. Five years later its capital surplus had grown
to 13½ million dollars. Alinco had also paid out nine million dollars in dividends.

Not only do rates for credit life insurance vary considerably, but the average consumer has no idea of what this insurance should cost. The rates the consumer pays may
range 300 per cent higher than premiums charged by
low-cost insurance companies. For example, a $1,000 loan

borrowed over a two-year period may include a credit life insurance policy which can cost you anywhere from $10 to $40, depending upon where you borrow and who has sold you the credit life. The benefits, whether you paid $10 or $40, are often identical. This variation in charges is often explained by whether you bought a group or individual policy. The group rate runs from 50 to 60 cents for each $100 of debt a year. Thus the premium charge for a group policy on a $1,000 loan to be paid over two years is $10 to $12. Most group policies are sold by the large all-purpose insurance companies. The individual policies, sold largely by the companies that specialize in credit life, cost $1 per $100 per year. Thus, the charge on the same $1,000 loan will come to $20. This charge can be doubled if you should be sold the latest gimmick in peace-of-mind insurance. Called "level benefit" insurance, this policy pays the full initial debt in event of death. It works this way. The debtor has borrowed $1,000 from a consumer finance company. He had paid back $400 when he died. Under a level benefit policy, the insurance firm will pay $600, the money he still owes, to the finance company. It will also pay $400 to the debtor's family, the sum the debtor had paid back to the lender. The premium charge for this policy is $2 per $100 per year or $40 on a $1,000 loan taken for two years.

The profits on individual and level benefit credit life insurance are immense. The amounts paid out in death benefit claims run about 25 cents per $100 per year. The overhead costs in selling such insurance ranges from an additional 5 cents to a high of 25 cents per $100. Thus when the debtor pays $1 for $100-worth of debt for a year under an individual policy the profit comes to 50 cents or a 100 per cent profit. Under a level benefit policy out of every $2 paid in premiums, the profits to the insurance company may range as high as $1.50. To put it another way, this is a profit of 300 per cent. The total profits from premiums paid for high-cost individual credit life has not been reported. However, the figure must run into millions of dollars. By the beginning of 1960 there was over five billion dollars of this kind of credit life insurance in force under eight million policies.

The frequent exorbitant charges made on credit life not only has meant lush profits for the insurer, but for the time seller himself. Unlike any other type of life insurance, credit life is sold to the public almost entirely through an agent who has no direct connection with the insurance business. Thus, the salesman for a peace-of-mind policy may be a car dealer, a small-loan operator, or a department store credit seller. The commissions received by the debt merchant for selling credit life may range as high as 40 per cent. (In Texas the loan sharks who sold credit life received commissions of 80 per cent.) The high commissions often given have resulted in a weird phenomenon called reverse competition. Instead of lowering the premium rates, the cost is kept high so that the debt merchant who sells the insurance may receive a maximum profit or commission. By combining the debt merchant's stake in high rates with some insurance companies' greed for excessive profits, the result is even higher premium charges.

Another abuse—and perhaps the most reprehensible—is that in a number of cases consumers are not even told that they are being sold credit life insurance. The premiums, frequently ranging as high as $100 or more, are skillfully hidden in a maze of finance, service and other insurance charges. The Association of Better Business Bureaus, an organization not easily given to alarm, delved into this problem in a recent nationwide survey. The survey noted that since 1958 the member bureaus have been experiencing a growing number of consumer complaints concerning credit life insurance. From January, 1959, through January, 1960, the Association proceeded to interview car purchasers whose names had been taken at random from public or credit records. Additional information was gathered from auto time buyers who complained to their local Better Business Bureaus. The combined result of both field and voluntary interviews showed that more than 58 per cent of the people had been sold credit life without even being told at the time of the transaction that they were purchasing such a policy.

Typical of the non-disclosure swindle was this affidavit signed by an angry debtor:

"The first time I learned of the cost of credit life insurance coverage was following the receipt of a post card from . . . Discount Corporation advising me that the cost of the physical damage insurance was $199. I then went to the office of . . . Discount Corporation inquiring about this insurance coverage, and the man in charge of the office told me that physical damage coverage was not the only insurance involved, that I owed $51.41 for credit life insurance. I then protested this charge. This man in charge of the office said his company had already purchased the insurance and it was mine, and if I wanted to cancel it, I could do so, but I would be short rated."

The Association of Better Business Bureaus also took note of the exorbitant charges often made in the sale of credit life. The report mentioned that the National Association of Insurance Commissioners—state officials charged with protecting the public in its insurance purchases—had recommended that if less than 50 per cent of the money taken in premiums is not paid in benefits then the rates are excessive. The N.A.I.C. went on to note that over 40 per cent of the non-specialty credit life companies were charging excessive rates in the latter part of 1950. Further, two-thirds of the companies who actually specialized in credit life had loss ratios of less than 40 per cent.

The N.A.I.C. report went on to state: "The statistics for individual credit life policies indicate that over half the companies reported loss ratios of less than 20 per cent (they should be 50 per cent or more) and almost one-third of the companies showed ratios of less than 10 per cent . . . Instances of high commission and fee payments are more evident in the individual coverages, with well over half of the companies paying in excess of 50 per cent for commissions and fees and such payments ranging into the 80 per cent and over category."

The Association of Better Business Bureaus noted that the debt merchant profiteering in credit life was charging exorbitant sums for a benefit the debtor didn't even know he was buying and in many instances had not even wanted. The Association went on to note: "These twin abuses in the sale of credit life insurance emphasize the need for disclosing through separate itemizations and specific charges that credit life insurance is included in a time purchase contract when such is the case."

During the middle and late nineteen-fifties a number of states became aware of the excesses that were resulting in the sale of credit life. So far at least twenty-two states have adopted in varying forms a model credit life insurance bill proposed by the National Association of Insurance Commissioners. Among other provisions, the bill calls for the disclosure to the time payer that he is purchasing credit life insurance. Although there was a sudden burst of legislative activity in 1959 to protect the purchaser of credit, this activity decreased in 1960. At this writing there are still twenty-eight states which do not require that a description of the types of insurance be indicated in the time sales agreement. In addition, no itemization of the separate charges for each type of insurance is required in thirty-four states. Further, twenty-one states do not have statutory controls which would prohibit combining the credit service charge with insurance charges. Thus, in half the states the seller of credit life is virtually given free rein under the law to take whatever advantage he wishes of the debtor.

It should be noted that a balancing force to the high rate charges are the low premium rates offered by some of the largest companies doing business in America. General Motors Acceptance Corporation, a subsidiary of General Motors, sells credit life insurance to auto buyers for 32½ cents per hundred. Prudential provides the insurance to G.M.A.C. under the world's largest insurance contract. The price G.M.A.C. pays is only 29 cents. Household Finance, which once sold credit life insurance at 45 cents a hundred, has raised the price to 60 cents. The giant small-loan company still supplies credit life free to customers in at least eight states. On the other hand, 90 per cent of the credit unions in the United States provide insurance that pays off the loan of the borrower in case of his death or permanent disability at no extra charge. The cost of the insurance is absorbed in the finance charges of 1 per cent per month on the unpaid balance or 12 per cent per annum simple interest.

Not all large big-name corporations, however, can pass up

the juicy profits offered in debt insurance. In February, 1959, Theodore O. Yntema, vice president in charge of finance at Ford Motor Company, told the Senate antitrust subcommittee on auto financing that the nation's second largest car manufacturer plans to set up its own sales finance company. One reason Yntema gave, was the high cost of credit insurance plans offered by the independent sales finance companies, compared to the inexpensive, stripped policy sold by G.M.A.C., General Motors' captive sales finance company. Here is an excerpt from Yntema's testimony:

> *Question:* In other words, none of those groups [the major independent sales finance companies] could compete with G.M.A.C.?
> *Yntema:* No, that is not what I said. I said they wouldn't.
> *Question:* They wouldn't?
> *Yntema:* They don't. Whether they can is something quite different. . . . We deal with C.I.T. [which finances 40 per cent of Ford cars bought on time]. We said, "G.M.A.C.'s rates are lower." They admitted they were lower, and we said, "Won't you meet this competition?" And they said, "No, we won't."
> *Senator Hart:* Did you go beyond that and ask why?
> *Yntema:* They are not particularly communicative. The answer is simple enough. They like to make 20 per cent after taxes, or 40 per cent before taxes.

L. W. Lundell, board chairman of Universal C.I.T. Credit Corporation, appeared before the Senate antitrust subcommittee two months later to answer Yntema's charges. He insisted that the $1 per hundred per year charged by C.I.T. for its credit insurance—67½ cents more per hundred than G.M.A.C.'s price—covered additional benefits.

Besides being protected by credit life, the purchaser of a C.I.T. plan also received disability debt insurance. Under this policy, an installment buyer must be disabled for four months before the insurance becomes effective. His payments are then refunded to him in cash and the insurance company continues to make his payments for as long as he remains disabled up to the end of his contract. This policy is sold to all persons under sixty-five. The C.I.T. board chairman went on to explain that the new C.I.T. plan, introduced in 1958, is optional, that it costs extra, and added that the customer is told about it in posters, pamphlets, notices, and in contracts. Counsel for the Senate subcommittee then asked the C.I.T. official this question: Does the auto dealer tell the customer that there is a difference between disability credit insurance and credit life insurance?

> *Lundell:* Customers are completely informed, probably by word of mouth, by little advertising handout pieces, things of that kind.
> *Question:* This advertising by C.I.T. you are speaking of?
> *Lundell:* Yes.
> *Question:* I am just wondering when the customer comes in, though, how the dealer presents it to him in terms of whether or not the customer does have a choice?
> *Lundell:* I am sure the customer is fully informed. This is a merchandising tool. This is an option. The May (1959) issue of *Reader's Digest* . . . has a wonderful Ford program of advertising. It covers some thirty-six pages of advertising telling the customer about automobiles, telling him about buying on time, telling him about everything. This advertisement here deals with optional equipment viewed as an investment . . . Well, now, Ford is selling equipment option. We are selling

peace of mind. We are selling peace of mind in the event of death. We are selling peace of mind in the event of disability.

According to the insurance experts, the peace-of-mind boom has just begun.

12 *The Car You Buy Is Not Your Own*

The variety and complexity of finance and insurance arrangements and the charges for them are such as almost to defy comprehension. It is impossible for the average buyer to appraise the rates for the finance and insurance services offered, as compared with alternatives available elsewhere.

Theodore O. Yntema, vice president in charge of finance, Ford Motor Company, testifying before the Senate hearing on auto financing.

The partner in a New Jersey auto dealership put it bluntly: "Cash? Let me tell you something. You couldn't buy one of our cars for cash if you wanted to. Every car we have here is sold on time." The auto dealer was perfectly sober. All he was doing was expressing the most important—and disturbing—phenomenon of the on-the-cuff explosion. As noted earlier, for the debt merchant the big profit comes not just from selling merchandise on credit, but through the sale of debt itself. Nowhere has this phenomenon become more apparent than in the marketing of cars. Indeed, in no other area is the battle for the debtor's dollar being fought with greater ferocity.

The size of the auto debt is the largest single factor in the entire consumer credit explosion. Over 17½ billion dollars was extended in credit for the purchase of new and used cars in 1960. This is equal to one-third of the total consumer debt. Of the six million new cars being sold yearly, about four million are bought on time. This means that consumers are paying more than two billion dollars a year in finance and insurance charges for new cars purchased on credit. The costs can be measured another way. According to Ford's Yntema two-thirds of all cars bought on time are paid for over a thirty-six-month period. On a new car bought on a typical thirty-six-month installment contract, the interest and insurance charges provided by an independent finance company average more than $600. These charges, he notes, are more than one-fifth and may amount to as much as one-quarter of the cash price.

The main reason most people go into debt to buy cars is that they simply can't afford to do otherwise. In an eleven-year study (1948-58) conducted by the Federal Reserve Board, over half of all spending units had less than $500 in liquid assets, that is money in a savings account, checking account or in U. S. Government savings bonds. At the top of the scale only about one out of five spending units reported liquid assets of $2,000 or more. The net result is that most people can just barely make the cash down payment. To be able to walk into an auto salesroom, plunk down a wad of one's own money and drive off with the year's new model still is a privilege enjoyed by only a few.

All this adds up to one conclusive fact: the sale of automobiles presents to the debt merchant a lush, ready-made market. How this market is being exploited—often to the detriment of the auto buyer—is the theme of this chapter.

The heart of the auto installment market is the sales finance business, an unusual operation that is distinct from almost all other forms of debt merchandising. The best way to define it would be to describe how it differs from the small-loan lender. In the small-loan business the lending institution deals directly with the borrower during the entire transaction. Further, the consumer borrows cash from the small-loan operator. By contrast, in the sales finance business no money is loaned to the consumer.* Instead, a sales finance company purchases the dealer's retail installment contract which arises when the dealer sells an automobile to the consumer. To put it another way, the dealer makes the initial contact with the customer. And it is with the dealer that the customer signs the contract. It is only after the dealer has sold the contract to the sales finance company that the finance company and the customer make contact. The customer then makes his installment payments to the sales finance company. In practice the sales finance company and the dealer work closely together. Before the customer can sign the contract, his credit rating must be checked and approved by the sales finance company. Further the contract signed by the customer is supplied by the sales finance company. In effect, the dealer is acting as the finance company's salesman, sort of a middleman debt merchant.

This somewhat complicated business got started shortly after the beginning of World War I. Despite early attempts to mass produce cars, they still remained beyond the reach of the average man's pocketbook. By 1914 the average value of all cars at the factory was $762. During the same year average annual wages for all industry came to about $627.

It became obvious that the only way to tap the mass market was through debt merchandising. The first serious attempt to finance automobiles was begun in 1915 by the

---

* A number of sales finance companies have recently entered the lucrative and growing small-loan business. By the end of July, 1960, the nation's sales finance companies had nearly one billion dollars outstanding in small loans. However, the small-loan operation is completely separate from sales financing.

Commercial Credit Company, today the second largest independent sales finance firm in the country. C.I.T., now the largest independent, followed a year later when an agreement was reached to assist Studebaker dealers to carry the contracts of installment buyers of Studebaker cars. According to C.I.T. this was the first contract between a financial institution and an automobile manufacturer contemplating a time-selling service on a national scale. In 1919, General Motors set up its own sales finance company, General Motors Acceptance Corporation. G.M.A.C. today has the distinction of being the largest sales finance company in existence, the largest captive finance company and the only remaining big sales finance company owned by an automobile manufacturer.

By the middle of the Jazz Age an essential part of the groundwork had been laid for the post-World War II carrousel in the debt merchants' paradise. However, before the big bang got under way other problems had to be worked out. One of the peculiarities of the automobile business is that it is the only industry where the manufacturer insists upon cash before delivering merchandise to the retailer. In other words, all those new cars you see in the salesroom as well as the car you order have already been paid for. And who lays out the capital for the purchase? Certainly not the dealer. In most instances he would never be able to maintain that kind of a reserve. The money the dealer pays the manufacturer for his stock almost invariably comes from the sales finance companies. Called floor planning or wholesaling, this money is loaned to the dealer at cost with no profit to the sales finance company. This wholesaling arrangement, however, does serve to compensate the finance company. For under the arrangement the dealer agrees to sell most of his highly lucrative retail installment contracts to the sales finance company. If the dealer should suddenly refuse to do so, then the sales finance company simply stops giving the dealer any more floor planning money. The dealer's choice: to look elsewhere or go out of business.

A second and most important tie between the dealer and the sales finance company directly affects how much the consumer pays in finance charges. This particular aspect of auto financing has been variously called dealer participation, dealer reserve, dealer's finders fee and finally the dealer's kickback. Originated by G.M.A.C. in 1925, it revolutionized auto debt merchandising. The auto debt merchant finds it as significant as the invention of the wheel. Unfortunately, in too many instances avaricious debt merchants have turned the wheel into a consumer's rack.

Prior to 1924 all that a sales finance company did for a dealer was to pay cash for the installment contract the dealer made with the customer. The dealer made no profit on this contract and at the same time assumed all the risks if the customer defaulted in his payments. Then, in 1924, the independent sales finance companies in order to get more business offered dealers a new deal. The independent sales finance companies agreed that they and not the dealer would be responsible if the customer failed to make payments. To offset the competitive advantage of the independent sales finance companies, G.M.A.C. raised the jackpot and offered to rebate to dealers a portion of the finance charges paid by the consumers. Within a year General Motors' captive finance company had increased its business by 225 per cent. Like news of a gold strike, the pulling power of the dealer's rebate or kickback swept through the sales finance industry until every company was offering it. Today, roughly half of the dealers' profits on the sale of new cars comes from the money he receives as part of his share in the consumers' finance charges. In fact, without this source of income hundreds of auto dealers would go bankrupt.

For the consumer, however, the rebate eventually meant not only unnecessary finance charges which he paid but that weird paradox known as reverse competition, where competition virtually leads to higher, not lower prices. The absurdity of this situation was succinctly summed up by William D. Warren, a University of Illinois Law Professor, in *The Yale Law Journal.*

"As already suggested," Professor Warren wrote, "because of the practice of dealer participation, increased competition among sales finance companies tends to exact not lower finance rates from the installment purchaser, but higher ones. The finance company that establishes a working arrangement with a dealer can confidently anticipate that the dealer will sell to it most of his retail installment contracts. And since dealers can, within limits, induce most buyers to finance on the terms offered by the dealer-chosen financer, sales finance companies and, to some extent, banks compete directly for the dealer's business rather than for the consumer's. But, common knowledge in the business, the rate of dealer participation is a principal factor in influencing the dealer's choice of financing agencies. To the extent that financers compete for the paper of dealers by increasing participation percentages, they exert a pressure tending to force finance rates upward."

The same conclusion was drawn in a report to the then Governor of Minnesota, Orville Freeman. The report, completed in 1959, was compiled by a committee of twenty-one business, legislative and social leaders, including three bank presidents, an auto dealer and the manager of the Minnesota League of Credit Unions. The Governor's committee declared:

"In our economic system the forces of competition tend to reduce prices and improve service to the consuming public. Therefore, it would appear that the intense competition in the automobile finance business should serve to lower the price of this service to the public. However, this is not the case, because competition is not effective at the rate charged the buyer. Instead, competition among financial institutions is directed toward the favor of the dealer rather than of the public. Thus, we see financial institutions vying with each other as to the amount of dealers' participation to be paid and which competition can and does cause the cost to the time buyer to go up. . . .

"This paradox, maximum competition resulting in higher costs to consumers, is at the heart of the problem."

Added to the debt merchant's reverse twist on prices is a nefarious scheme called the pack. To understand how the pack works, it is first necessary to realize that when you buy a car on time the finance rate you pay may not be the same as the rate paid by your neighbor. Some finance companies have as many as eight charts which spell out the finance charges the dealer will include in figuring out your contract. These rate charts may range from over 11 per cent to more than 17 per cent true annual interest. The ostensible purpose for the different rates is that a dealer may want to levy a higher finance charge if the customer is a poor risk. In practice, however, the auto dealer may use the higher rate chart simply because the larger finance charge will mean more money in his pocket.

For example, let's assume you want to buy a new car whose retail price is $3,000. The dealer will give you $1,200 as the trade-in price for your old car. You now owe the dealer $1,800. Now tack on another $200 for auto insurance, plus $100 more for credit life insurance. The final price is $2,100. Like most other time buyers, you want to take thirty-six months to pay. The dealer, if he is so minded, can pull out a so-called 5 per cent rate chart. Your finance charges will come to $315 ($105 a year for three years). Not too bad. But let's assume the dealer figures you for a sucker. Instead of using the 5 per cent rate chart, he decides to use the 8 per cent rate chart. Your finance charges are now $504. Or he may even try the 9 per cent rate chart if he thinks he can get away with it and the sales finance company is unscrupulous enough to accept it. Your finance charges have just climbed another $63 to $567. Of course these are only rate charts for new cars. Rates used for second-hand cars are invariably higher. For old used cars rate charts may range from 24 to 34 per cent true annual interest.

Here is where the sales finance company comes in. The finance company keeps a portion of the charges paid by the consumer. This is usually a fixed percentage. Thus, in the purchase of a new car where the dealer uses a 5 per cent rate chart, the sales finance company may hold the entire amount. With a 6 per cent rate, the dealer gets 1 per cent, the sales finance company 5. A 9 per cent rate gives the dealer 4 per cent. The sales finance company again keeps 5. Using the above example, this means in dollars that with a finance charge of $315 (based on a 5 per cent rate chart) the sales finance keeps the entire amount. A finance charge of $378 (based on a 6 per cent rate chart) gives the dealer $63, the sales finance company $315. Finally, a finance charge of $567 (using a 9 per cent rate chart) gives the dealer $252, the sales finance company again $315.

Actually this is not all the dealer receives. The sales finance company puts aside a certain amount of the sum it keeps in the dealer's reserve, mentioned previously. The purpose of the reserve is to protect the sales finance company and the dealer in case the car buyer defaults in his payments. Thus, if the sales finance company sets a 5 per cent figure as the amount it will keep, one-fifth of that may be set aside and put into the dealer's reserve. This means that out of the $315 originally kept by the sales finance company, $63 (or one-fifth) is put in the dealer's reserve. Eventually most or all of that $63 will be rebated to the dealer. To sum up, the dealer may receive a portion or all of the reserve plus part of the finance charge paid by the customer.

We now come to the definition of the pack. It simply means that the dealer sells to the unsuspecting customer the highest finance charge he can get away with. The finance company, when it buys the contract from the dealer, keeps the standard amount, say $315 as used in the examples above, and returns the rest to the dealer. Thus, the dealer may receive as much as $252 from the pack price plus $63 from the dealer's reserve or kickback.

The pack frequently is hidden in the monthly payments quoted the customer. Thus, the man who owes the auto dealer $2,100 over a thirty-six-month period may not realize he is overpaying $189 in finance charges—the difference between a 6 per cent and 9 per cent rate. For that additional $189, when broken down into thirty-six monthly payments, comes to $5.25 a month, an insignificant sum that the gulli-

ble car buyer is not even aware of. This is invariably true
when no finance charge or rate is quoted even though it is
charged.

Although most sales finance companies and dealers frown
at least in public on the pack, its use is undoubtedly widespread. The following exchange perhaps best sums up the
problem the consumer faces. This colloquy took place during the recent Senate hearing on the consumer credit labeling bill. The participants are Senator Paul Douglas, a spon-
sor of the bill, and John L. O'Brien, president of the Better
Business Bureau of Greater St. Louis.

Senator Douglas: What I mean is, since the dealer does not
assume the risk (when the auto buyer defaults) . . . the dealer
really performs no economic function to justify the return,
except getting business.

O'Brien: The finder's fee is the only function he performs
. . . By now, it is in this fashion that the original principle has
long since been lost sight of. It is now a finder's fee operation, as
you so aptly term it, sir.

Senator Douglas: All right.

O'Brien: Shall I continue?

Senator Douglas: Yes.

O'Brien: Most finance firms prepared rate charts showing
the amount of monthly payments which would be required to
pay off a given unpaid balance over a period of months as a
means of assisting the dealer in figuring a customer's obligation
quickly and easily. Customarily these companies also provided
the dealers with several rate charts which carried increasingly
higher rates, which were supposed to be based on the amount of
risk which the company and/or the dealer would be assuming in
the case of progressively older cars, which because of the greater
risk, would command a higher rate. Persons with poor credit
were also supposed to pay a higher rate to cover the company's

probable losses. Some charts included insurance coverage, some did not. Seldom could the purchaser tell what he was getting. So often, as we shall see later, a multiplicity of such rate charts were provided the dealer and he could simply select whichever one best suited his needs, or the gullibility of his customer, and use it to convince his customer that his total obligation should be exactly what the rate chart called for. In such cases, by prearrangement with certain unscrupulous finance companies, the company would agree to buy from the dealer at the prearranged discount rate, whatever customer time paper the dealer chose to sell, and rebate to him any amount over the preagreed discount rate. This became known as "the pack." Unhappily, it still goes on today in many states where no control is exerted over time finance contracts of this type.

Senator Douglas: Just a minute, Mr. O'Brien. This is a very serious charge that you are making. Do you mean to say what the finance company does is to give the dealer a hunting license to go out and get as high finance charges as he can from the individual buyer and then he gets everything over a basic amount? He gets a percentage and, then, everything over a basic given amount?

O'Brien: I do.

Senator Douglas: This is based on a wide study on your part?

O'Brien: Yes, sir.

Although several states attempted to control the dealer's kickback, this practice is regulated only in Ohio and Michigan. About thirty states have set maximum finance rates dealers can charge auto buyers. These laws, however, do not exert any control over the kickback the dealer receives out of the reserve held by the sales finance company. Further, although they do limit the size of the pack, the laws do not eliminate it. In fact, in some states the finance charges fixed by the law are so exorbitant that they virtually legalize the packing of the unscrupulous dealer.

The kickback and the pack are not the only plums plucked from the consumer's pocket by the debt merchant. Time selling has other virtues—at least for the manufacturer and dealer—whereby the cash price soars upward without the consumer having the foggiest notion that he is paying more. This proved particularly true during the nineteenfifties when the extension of the payment period served as a handy cloak to hide and obscure major auto price increases.

The three years currently allowed for repayments undoubtedly would have shocked the old-fashioned debt merchants right out of their wicker chairs. Way back in 1916 when C.I.T. joined the great experiment, the maximum term was eight months. During the nineteen-twenties it grew to one year; during the nineteen-thirties to eighteen months, and by the late nineteen-forties it had been extended to two years. Then in the nineteen-fifties time periods stretched like new elastic. By 1954 the payment periods of nearly half of all new cars financed by the four largest companies were extended beyond two years. Today twothirds of all new cars bought on time have a three-year time payment.

As time payments stretched into the never-never, prices soared. The total cost to the buyer of a Chevrolet (assuming a 40 per cent down payment computed on car, optional equipment and freight) rose from $2,855 in 1955 to $3,466 in 1958, an increase of $611. A simple recalculation shows how this increase was handled so that the rise in costs to a time buyer appeared as a lowering of prices. If the 1955 Chevrolet had been financed for twenty-four months at the rate then prevailing the monthly payments came to $74.67. By increasing the down payment by $210 and extending the monthly payments to thirty, financing of a 1958 Chevrolet resulted in a monthly payment of $74.59. *This is eight cents per month less than the 1955 monthly payments. Thus, an increase in total cost of over $600 was completely absorbed by a $210 increase in the down payment and an extension of six more monthly payments.*

Not surprisingly, in the last ten years finance charges have jumped the fastest of all auto costs. The reasons are four-fold: the rise in price of the car, higher interest rates, smaller down payments and, most important, longer terms. For example, a typical finance charge on a Ford Fairlane in 1960 came to $130 a year. This was about four times an estimated $30 finance charge paid per year on the 1950 Ford. The increase in the finance charges is further compounded by the extension of the time periods. Where the typical Ford buyer on a two-year contract paid only $60 in finance charges in 1950, he now pays $390 over a three-year period. This is a 550 per cent increase in finance charges. (The introduction of the compacts has brought the time buyer some relief. The interest costs are generally lower because the compact is usually cheaper. This holds true, however, only if the so-called economy-sized cars and the standard autos are financed on the same time and interest terms. It should also be noted that the savings on compacts effects only a minority of American car buyers. While a third of the U. S. market now goes to compacts and foreign cars, the remainder still consists of standard models.)

Ironically, those easy, endless payments have stretched like rubber money to the point where the full impact of the price increases are at last becoming noticeable to the discerning car buyer. It can all be summed up by what is happily known as the thirty-six-month wall. This simply means that at least during the early nineteen-sixties, finance terms on new cars will not go beyond three years. The thirty-six-month limit does not grow out of a sudden stroke of conscience whereby the dealers, sales finance companies and banks feel that the price of consumer debt must end somewhere. On the contrary, the three-year limit is derived from a single economic fact: the auto debt merchants cannot afford a further extension of the payment periods. Here is why. Suppose you have just bought a new car from Happy Harry, America's friendly car dealer. You turn on the ignition, step on the accelerator and drive out of the show-room. By the time you reach the street the value of your car has just depreciated by 20 per cent. That means if the car was worth $3,000 when you stepped into it, its value had dropped to $2,400 by the time you reached the curb. By the end of the third year it would be worth about $1,000. To put it another way, assume a 25 per cent down payment and thirty-six monthly payments, the buyer owes more than the car's resale value for more than a year and a quarter. Extending the finance period to forty-two months would leave the buyer owing more than the resale value for a year and three quarters. Under these circumstances it would be to the buyer's self-interest to let his car be repossessed and for him to use the amount still owed for the purchase of a newer used car. We have virtually reached the point where the car buyer whose payments are stretched over a long enough period gets more value for his money if he defaults and then invests the remaining money he owes in another car.

This apparently explains in part the dead beat experience of General Motors Acceptance Corporation. The giant sales finance company reports that more than 80 per cent of its new car repossessions are made on buyers who have completed less than ten monthly payments. This credit in wonderland phenomenon may also explain the fantastic rise in new car repossessions during the last decade, when time payments were stretched from two to three years. In 1948, G.M.A.C.'s new car repossessions numbered only 549. By 1957, they had soared to 50,652, an increase of over 9,000 per cent. As we enter the nineteen-sixties, sales finance companies, dealers and banks may be repossessing as many as 200,000 new cars a year. Since repossessions almost invariably result in a loss to the finance institution, it is understandable why most companies insist on the thirty-six-month wall. This means that the auto industry can no longer camouflage price increases by extending time payments. Prices, however, are likely to rise again. If buyers' resistance grows great enough, it is conceivable that to maintain or expand the market the auto industry will breach the wall and offer a forty-two-month or forty-eight-month payment period. For the consumer, rarely a winner, it will mean even greater finance charges. For the debt merchants it will mean thousands of additional car repossessions. And for the one out of every seven people in the country who owe their livelihood directly or indirectly to the motor car industry, it could eventually mean an auto glut that would result in perhaps the most disturbing recession since the aftermath of World War II.

However gloomy the outlook may appear, the auto industry is currently engaged in another matter—who will be gorged on the auto debt cake. The battle that is taking place is one of the most important, not only affecting consumer credit but the structure of the free enterprise system itself. The major participants in this battle are the giant auto manufacturers, namely General Motors, Ford and Chrysler; the nation's four hundred-odd sales finance companies, and Congress. The stakes involved: the hundreds of millions of dollars Ford and Chrysler would receive through the creation of their own captive sales finance companies. These sales finance companies would be identical to General Motors' own captive, General Motors Acceptance Corporation.

For the mammoth debt merchant the profits derived from time selling stagger the ordinary mortal. Net income earned by General Motors' G.M.A.C. for just three years (1957 through 1959) totaled over 144 million dollars. This includes profits from the operations of Motors Insurance Corporation, the insurance affiliate of G.M.A.C.*

Although profits for the large independent sales finance companies have not been as stupendous as G.M.A.C.'s, they have been substantial. The prospects of auto debt merchandising on a gigantic scale were dramatically summarized by Ford's Yntema at the Senate anti-trust and monopoly hearings on auto financing legislation. The Ford official quoted the executive vice president of a successful sales

---

* Dealers also benefit from the sale of tie-in insurance. They received insurance commissions of between 25 and 30 per cent of the premiums paid on collision policies and 15 to 20 per cent on credit life and personal accident insurance. For example, G.M.A.C. collects the insurance premium from the auto buyer and then remits the commissions to the dealer through M.I.C. Professor Warren notes in the April, 1959, issue of *The Yale Law Journal:* "G.M.A.C. has advertised to its dealers that insurance is a part of a 'one package plan' that enables them to make more profit dealing with G.M.A.C. than with banks. It has advertised to the public that one of the advantages of doing business with G.M.A.C. is that it offers insurance protection as part of a 'one package' transaction."

finance company: "I have lain awake nights trying to find out what is wrong with this [sales finance] business. I can't find anything wrong with it. It is a profit making business. I have made more money in this business than I ever dreamed I would make. Everybody who has been in it for twenty years has made at least a million dollars, and most of them have made a lot more. It is a low-risk business and a high-return business."

For Ford and Chrysler the creation of captive finance companies would mean not only great financial rewards for themselves but greater control over their franchised dealers. It would also mean that by joining General Motors, the Big Three auto producers would control 90 per cent of all new car registrations and 68 per cent of the financing of the cars of all three. Senator Kefauver, in his statement that opened the 1959 anti-monopoly hearings on auto financing legislation, summed up the reasons why he and Senator O'Mahoney proposed bills that would prohibit auto manufacturers from maintaining their own sales finance companies:

> This is not the first time the solution of the problem of the control of financing of automobiles by automobile manufacturers has been undertaken by the antitrust approach. In May 1938, General Motors, Ford, and Chrysler were indicted under the Sherman Act for alleged coercion of their dealers to finance car sales through the finance firm owned by the manufacturer. Civil cases also were filed seeking divestiture of the finance businesses from each. Chrysler and Ford consented to divestiture of their finance firms and the criminal cases against them were dismissed.
>
> General Motors went to trial in the criminal case in 1939,

was convicted and fined. Its civil case was finally settled by consent decree in 1952. Divorcement of General Motors Acceptance Corporation from General Motors was not obtained in the decree. Thus, General Motors and G.M.A.C. remained joined together, which placed Ford and Chrysler at a greater disadvantage as competitors than before the litigation began. Instead of freeing the industry from monopolistic control, the largest company was left with a stronger power than it had previously enjoyed. In order to alleviate this unfairness and increased tendency to monopoly, the courts have afforded an opportunity to Ford and Chrysler to again enter the financing business. Recently Ford announced its intention of re-entering the finance business and it has been rumored that Chrysler is considering doing the same.

It therefore appears that very soon we will be exactly where we were in 1938 in spite of approximately twenty years of litigation under existing antitrust laws. Instead of removing the monopoly power from the automobile industry and the finance and insurance business, it has gone on growing on the part of General Motors and now threatens the same results as to Chrysler and Ford.

Ford insists that its only desire to re-enter the sales finance business is to give dealers and consumers financing plans that are competitive with those offered by G.M.A.C. Yntema, during his testimony, declared that a time buyer purchasing his car through G.M.A.C. instead of through an independent company saves from $65 to $150. Among the additional costs tacked on by the independents, he said, is the so-called "package charge" which normally includes credit life and disability insurance, a bail bond certificate, a travel emergency certificate and towing and labor coverage. On a thirty-two-month contract, he added, this comes to at least $70 in "frills and fluff."

However, Paul C. Jones, president of American Securities Division of ASC Corporation, disagreed with Yntema's defense of G.M.A.C. Jones testified: "He (Yntema) repeatedly states that he wants this company (a Ford sales finance company) operated like G.M.A.C. who has a clean, streamlined operation without fluff. We are filing rate charts of G.M.A.C. to show that they enter into the competitive practice of packing the finance charge which is exactly what Yntema talks about when he mentions fluff. The fluff he referred to with respect to C.I.T. and connected with credit life and accident policy, or in other words a motor club package, is merely a pack masquerading as a package. It is identical with the unmasqueraded pack of G.M.A.C."

The president of G.M.A.C., Charles G. Stradella, told the same Senate antimonopoly subcommittee in 1958, that G.M.'s captive sales finance company purchases contracts for new cars financed at the 9 per cent rate where it is legal.

What this means is that G.M.'s dealers can operate under a pack. In other words the "fluff" sold by the independent sales finance companies can be made up in the high finance rates General Motors' dealers are permitted to charge with the approval of G.M.A.C.

Thus, for the consumer, there is no advantage in a combine of automotive manufacturer, dealer and sales finance company. The costs to the time payer are as high or higher. But there is yet another advantage to the auto manufacturer which owns its own sales finance company, the control and monopolization of its franchised dealers. Let us again turn to the testimony of Paul C. Jones:

The G.M. dealer receives five incomes controlled by G.M. and its subsidiaries, an exclusive General Motors privilege. They are (1) the markup on the new car (2) the normal reserve for losses on time sales set up on the books of G.M.A.C. (3) the overage or pack charged to time buyers when the charges reach or approach the maximum set by law, and such overage is then credited to or paid to the dealer by G.M.A.C. (4) the commission paid auto dealers on insurance included and paid for in the time sale contract (5) the income, so long as the dealer remains a G.M. dealer, from the repairs and parts replacements under losses under such policies.

Under the G.M. mobility or subsidy plan, all these incomes are under G.M. control and passed on to the dealer from G.M. or its subsidiaries. With an understanding of this, it becomes clear why G.M.A.C. with all its freak advantages of leverage, low money costs, and practically no acquisition costs, permits high charges to the public. The maximum rates simply generate the overages or packs paid by the time buyers. G.M.A.C. then becomes the source of this pocket of income for the dealer. This along with the other four pocketbooks enables G.M. to control and hold the G.M. dealers from going to other manufacturers. It practically eliminates dealer turnover from G.M. to other manufacturers and attracts the best dealers from the other manufacturers.

Ford would like to have these advantages and that is why they feel they must have their own finance and insurance subsidiary unless G.M.A.C. is divorced from G.M.

Perhaps even more important is the effect a Big Three sales finance combine would have on the competitive free enterprise system. It would give General Motors, Ford and Chrysler so many advantages over their smaller competitors —American Motors and Studebaker—that these two motorcar manufacturers could easily be driven out of business.

Furthermore, it could create a combine so powerful and vast in its holding that administered or parallel prices could be matched by higher, fixed finance rates.

For the debt merchants of Detroit the future is bright. For the consumer it is indeed frightening.

13 *A Summing Up*

One wonders, inevitably, about the tensions associated with debt creation on such a massive scale.
The legacy of wants, which are themselves inspired,
are the bills which descend like the winter snow on
those who are buying on the installment plan. By
millions of hearths throughout the land it is known
that when these harbingers arrive the repossession
man cannot be far behind. Can the bill collector be
the central figure in the good society?

John Kenneth Galbraith in The Affluent Society
(*Houghton Mifflin Co. 1958*)

It is the thesis of this book that the American consumer who
buys on credit is often being abused and deceived and in
some instances outrageously swindled. It does not follow,
however, that debt in itself is wrong. No one can dispute the
fact that the widespread use of credit in the United States
has helped raise our standard of living beyond the attain-
ments of any other peoples anywhere in the world. Consumer debt has not only meant more material comfort for
more people, but more jobs through increased production.

A dramatic illustration of the important, indeed vital
role, consumer credit plays in our economic well-being can
be shown by examining what the immediate effect would
be if, starting in the fall of 1961, Americans were no longer
allowed to buy cars on time. First of all, there would be at
least a 50 per cent reduction in the number of cars manu-
factured. In turn, this would mean America would produce
8 per cent less steel, 24 per cent less malleable iron, 21 per

cent less lead, 15 per cent less zinc, 10 per cent less nickel and 31 per cent less synthetic rubber. In terms of jobs it could mean unemployment for 370,000 wage earners who make motor vehicles and parts. The work force of two million people engaged in automotive sales and servicing might be cut by a third. Probably one hundred thousand petroleum workers would no longer have jobs. Finally, the havoc that would result in our economy in general would make any of the post-World War II recessions appear as years of almost unbounded prosperity. In effect, debt buying is neither a fad nor experiment but a necessity. Without it, America would not continue to grow.

Nor should the value of consumer credit be measured just by the fact that it has become an integral part of our existence. Credit, if used properly, serves as an important democratizing force. Stated in its simplest terms, people with modest incomes simply do not have the cash with which to purchase furniture, TV sets, refrigerators, cars, washing machines. Despite the theories of the anti-materialist school, it does not seem to me inherently evil that people desire and buy more goods and services which give them more comfort and leisure. Time buying does afford low-income couples greater opportunity to marry earlier, raise families while they are still young, and to enjoy many of the benefits which the upper-income couple can virtually take for granted. To pay while one consumes—and that is the definition of buying on time—is no less a virtue than paying cash.

Finally, consumer credit offers thousands of people opportunities they might not otherwise experience. One of the major airlines, for example, discovered that more than 80 per cent of its pay-later customers had actually never flown before. Further, the typical Fly-Now, Pay-Later customer earns $4,800, works as a skilled, semi-skilled or unskilled worker. It seems absurd to believe that the thrill and joy of visiting other lands should be reserved for the few.

Certainly the most important contribution consumer credit can make is to help qualified youngsters obtain a college education which they might not otherwise be able to afford. According to the University of Michigan Survey Research Center the average annual expenses of unmarried students during 1959-60 came to $1,540. Of this amount scholarships accounted for only $130. Student earnings and miscellaneous sources supplied $470. It was the parents who paid the biggest part, $940 or 60 per cent of the total expenses. The Michigan Survey Center figures are actually minimal. The cost of sending youngsters to the higher-priced private colleges may mean an annual expenditure of $2,000 to $2,500, or $8,000 to $10,000 for a four-year Liberal Arts education. Even more alarming is the prediction made by the U. S. Office of Education which expects that by 1970 four years at a public institution may cost as much as $13,600. Attendance at a private college may mean a student and his family will have to pay as much as $18,400—prohibitive sums for most families.

To meet this need some of the more responsible lending institutions have originated plans whereby families can borrow as much as $10,000 for each youngster's education. The interest rates generally are lower than those charged for personal loans. The most common repayment terms for a four-year college loan is six years. In addition, most plans provide credit life insurance at either a nominal cost or the cost is included in the finance charges. The biggest program so far is C.I.T.'s Tuition Plan, Inc., which, in the past four years, has served 75,000 families. Where C.I.T.'s Tuition Plan is currently restricted to some three hundred colleges and universities, Education Funds, Inc., set up by Household Finance Corporation, has no limitations as to the school the youngster attends. Further, E.F.I. strongly recommends in the material it sends to parents that they should repay the loan as quickly as possible so they can save on the financing charges.

Besides the Tuition Plan and E.F.I. there are over one hundred banks throughout the nation that have installed educational credit programs. These plans can only be used by people who live in the state or community where the bank is located. However, the banks charge simple annual interest rates of between 6 and 8 per cent, considerably lower than the charges made on personal bank loans and a slight savings when compared to most other forms of educational credit. According to the American Bankers Association, banks are now announcing new plans weekly. There is no question that a growing segment of the consumer credit industry is attempting to fulfill a pressing, indeed dire need at a minimal cost. In 1959, an estimated $100 million was borrowed by parents to pay for their youngsters' college educations. Although this is only one-fifth of the one cent of every dollar of consumer credit extended, the amount of money available for educational loans is growing rapidly.

Despite the varied contributions consumer credit can and is making to our social well-being, there still remains the inescapable conclusion that too many people are being sold more debt than they can afford at exorbitant prices of which they are not even aware. It seems strange that in this era of relative prosperity more than twice as many families went bankrupt during 1959 than during the height of the Depression. This does not mean that we have become so overloaded with debt that the economy itself is in danger of collapsing. However, the continuous surge of time buying can create economic instability.

Only a few economists, for example, would deny that the too rapid expansion of auto debt in 1955 heightened and may have even precipitated the 1957-58 recession. By 1955 auto finance terms were loosened and repayment periods were made easier. As one Senate Judiciary subcommittee investigating auto prices noted, "Given an urge to buy on the part of the public, a very active urge to sell on the part of the auto manufacturers and dealers, and the willing cooperation on the part of the financing agencies, new car sales made history in 1955. There is some basis for believing they made too much history." Not only did Americans buy 7½ million new cars in 1955, a figure yet to be equaled, but they committed themselves to so much debt that their purchasing power was sharply constricted during the next two to three years. Paul A. Samuelson, an M.I.T. economist, writing in *The New York Times Magazine*, summed it up: "So long as the consumer can increase or decrease his consumption expenditures by a twist of his pen, the unavoidable instability of business investment and government defense spending may be compounded by similar consumer instability."*

* A great debate has raged over whether the federal government should attempt to control the consumer credit explosion. In concluding his article Samuelson summed up the issues involved and then made the following suggestion: "Should the new Congress re-enact selective credit controls over consumer finance, with all the administrative headache and infringements on individual liberties that such controls imply? Or should we tolerate extra instabilities in consumption spending as a necessary evil, to be minimized, however imperfectly, by conventional monetary policies?

"Speaking for myself, I would prefer enactment of stand-by powers over

There remains a question of even graver concern than the disturbing and unsettling effect consumer credit has on the economy. That question involves the changing purpose of consumer debt itself. As noted earlier the original function of consumer credit was to sell merchandise and services. Credit, in this sense, had a social purpose whereby the goods or services bought on time had some human use. This was the ultimate function. Among other things it helped in the mass distribution of goods and raised the standard of living. During the past decade, however, sellers of credit discovered more profit could be derived from debt itself so that the sale of merchandise and goods became subordinated to the sale of credit. For the consumer this meant that he was buying something which had no function, no use, no purpose. For the debt merchant it meant easy profits. In effect, the debt merchants found that by using refrigerators, cars, TV sets, and furniture as bait they were able to sell debt on a grand scale.

The phenomenon of debt merchandising in part explains why the consumer is being subjected to a constant pounding to Buy Now, Pay Later. This daily twenty-four-hour entreaty over the airwaves, the TV screens and in the daily newspapers has supplied much of the powder in the consumer credit explosion. Debt selling, of course, is not the only reason we have been able to indulge ourselves in an on-the-cuff binge after World War II. The removal of federal consumer credit restrictions, the release of factories for the production of consumer goods, the increase in personal

consumer credit, but with the definite understanding that the Federal Reserve is to reserve such weapons for acute and presumably short-term emergencies that might arise in the future."

income, all are crucial elements in the extraordinary rise in credit buying. Yet it is these factors combined with the endless bombardment of debt merchandising that are producing hardship, anguish and degradation for many. The result is reflected in the phenomenal rise in family bankruptcies, the startling increase and widespread use of wage attachments and the fourfold rise in debt consolidation, the most rapidly growing type of consumer debt. One cannot avoid the conclusion that a new class—the indigent debtor— is emerging in America. This class is made up of people from all walks of life with a wide variety of incomes who have been overloaded and oversold debts they are unable to pay.

Equally alarming is the effect an excess of on-the-cuff living has on our sense of proportion and values. It is not that we want too many comforts—Lord knows there is nothing wrong with a high standard of living—but that we must have all of them now, this minute. In effect, we are reacting to the wonderland of easy credit the way a child reacts to a stick of candy which is constantly waved before his eyes. And like the child who can't resist we consume more debt than we can digest simply because we are losing our will power to wait for the things we want.

One result of this rush toward debt is a shocking kind of personal economic immaturity, an inability to plan for future emergencies and family needs. A typical expression of this phenomenon can be found in the results of a recent Ford Foundation study of a representative group of parents expecting to send their children to college. The survey showed that 60 per cent had not saved any money for their youngsters' education and the 40 per cent who were putting money away had saved an average of only $150 a year. This inability to save is reflected again by the fact that during the past decade consumer installment loans made from banks rose four times as fast as deposits.

It is one of the paradoxes of debt merchandising that it is actually being sold to people as a form of savings. It is not uncommon, for example, for people to buy an item on time even though they have sufficient savings in the bank to pay for it. A reason often given is that they simply would not have the will power to replace the money they had spent. However, they have no trouble in putting money aside for the bill collector simply because they know this is a debt they owe and are forced to pay. Although paying cash may save them considerable sums of money, this advantage to their own pocketbook is either ignored or considered unimportant. Amazingly, saving through time buying, a contradiction in terms, is one of the debt merchants' most effective selling weapons.

The most disturbing aspect of debt merchandising is that it is generally based on deception. The deception varies in degree and amount, but it occurs almost every time someone is sold debt. Moreover, what really jars the moral nerve is that much of this deception is now considered normal behavior by most of the nation's respected and respectable business institutions. This statement undoubtedly would be challenged by every debt merchant with the power of speech. The argument offered, and I've listened to it many times, is that there are now one hundred million people in the United States who at this very moment are paying for something they bought on time. Is it possible, the argument runs, that one hundred million people do not know what they are doing? Do you mean to say we are a nation of fools? My answer is that we are not fools, but that we are being fooled, singularly and collectively. And the sooner we recognize it the better off we will be.

Not only the average citizen, but even the most sophisticated consumer is completely incapable of calculating the cost of credit. The myriad charges, many of them hidden, the infinite ways in which finance rates are presented, the continual emphasis on the amount of the monthly payments, all of these things are lulling us with a false sense of economy and, more important, are turning us into a nation of consumer idiots. We buy without asking how much and pay without question. And the reason we don't know how much we are paying for debt is that those who sell it refuse to divulge what it costs in terms that we can truly comprehend. For the debt merchants—and I am including many of our most august banks, department stores, sales finance companies and small-loan firms—this means profits made at the expense of an ignorant and uninformed citizenry. It is deception on a grand scale and it has no place in our free enterprise system.

Indeed, one of the ironies of debt merchandising is that it is eroding the system we call free competition. By not telling the consumer the true cost of credit, the debt merchants in effect have removed competition from the market place. The irony is even heightened by the revolutionary changes that have taken place in the structure of the consumer credit market. Today, more than ever before, the consumer has an increasing number of different sources from which he can buy or borrow on time. Yet the consumer of the nineteen-sixties is totally incapable of taking advantage of the variety of credit institutions that in fact exist. Unable to compare the cost of credit, he simply cannot exercise any sort of intelligent choice.

The final judgment, and it is severe, is that the sanctimonious and even hypocritical attitude so frequently expressed by the reputable debt merchants blurs the moral atmosphere, making it possible for the unscrupulous credit gouger to thrive. Typical of this attitude was the statement made to me by the executive of a merchants' association who characterized all criticism of teen-age debt as "vicious." Debt for children, he insisted, teaches them credit responsibility. It was not until I noted that teen-age debt builds store loyalty, that he admitted that selling debt to youngsters involves some pecuniary gain.

The executive's statement, interestingly, was made a few months after Earl B. Schwulst, president of the Bowery Savings Bank in New York, offered his opinion of teen-age debt before the Douglas Committee. "I think," he declared, "this (selling credit to youngsters) is something like teaching the young to use narcotics. I think it is very bad, very bad, indeed. I think the merchants and the merchants' associations ought to repudiate this sort of thing. It is this kind of thing which gives the Russians ammunition against our private enterprise system, saying that all we are interested in is building up volume and anything for the buck. This is bad, unqualifiedly bad, in my judgment."

I submit that teen-age debt, though more obviously shocking in its implications, is on the same amoral plane as the "pack," overloading low- and middle-income families with debt, hiding the cost of credit and charging exorbitant premiums for "peace-of-mind insurance." I believe it is this atmosphere of "the fast buck" that breeds such activities as described in the final report of the California Senate Judiciary Committee's investigation of wiretapping. In a summary of its findings the California wiretap committee noted under the subheading: *Listening to potential customers discuss what characteristics appeal to them.* "This has been done so that a sales person can then move in and make the sale more effectively. In the Los Angeles area several used-car dealers have maintained bugged rooms where they would let a couple, for example, talk over 'privately' what car they liked or could afford to buy; then the salesman comes in, armed with the information."

It seems to me that we can no longer as individuals and people countenance such an atmosphere of deception, sharp practices and, on too frequent occasions, unmitigated fraud. Fortunately, there are a number of concrete steps which I believe we can take to preserve not only our individual values and dignity but, equally important, the moral and social well-being of the community.

Back a Federal Consumer Credit Labeling Bill. Passage of this measure would make it mandatory for all sellers of credit to inform the purchaser of the cost of the finance charges in dollars and cents and in terms of simple annual interest. A bill (S. 2755) which includes these provisions was proposed by Senator Paul H. Douglas and others during the second session of the Eighty-sixth Congress. Hearings were held in the spring of 1960. Testimony, which I have so liberally quoted, pointed up the overwhelming need for its passage. The measure, however, has not become law as of this writing. Senator Douglas plans to reintroduce the bill in the 1961 session of Congress.

A major objection to the bill is that there are so many different ways of calculating simple interest that even mathematicians would come up with a variety of answers. This criticism of the bill is valid for the moment. However, solutions to similar problems have been made time and again. For example, it wasn't so long ago that the foot was defined as the length of the king's pedal extremity. As a result, measurements differed not only from province to province but from merchant to merchant. A similar problem faced man when he wanted to standardize weights and measures. This problem, however, was solved when scientists and governments jointly arrived at a series of standard measurements that were acceptable. A universal definition of simple annual interest can also be reached if mathematicians, credit sellers, economists and government officials agreed to work it out. There is no doubt that some yardstick is needed if consumers hope to compare credit costs. Even though no universally accepted standard formula for simple annual interest has been chosen, the consumer would still benefit considerably if he applied one of the formulas in calculating the comparative costs of credit. (See Appendix for sample formulas.) In many instances the variations in the answers are slight. It would appear absurd to insist that in an age when man is solving the mathematical calculations that will take him to the moon, he is incapable of agreeing on a standard formula that would measure the price he pays for debt.

As *Consumer Reports* noted: "To be sure, a formula which tends to minimize the interest charge, as opposed to one which does not, would be less desirable. But a universal standard for the expression of credit charges is the prime objective. Without it, consumers cannot shop for credit as they do for goods and they must venture unprotected into a consumer credit market where the price for this service, concealed by misleading statements of cost, varies from a low of 8 to 10 per cent in true annual interest terms up to high above the 129.5 per cent calculated by one of Senator Bennett's panel." (The Senator from Utah is one of the Douglas Bill's more forceful critics.)

Prohibit Car Manufacturers from Financing Automobiles. Legislation was proposed in the first session of the Eighty-sixth Congress that would break up the General Motors-G.M.A.C. combine and prevent Ford and Chrysler from starting their own captive sales finance companies. Hearings were held in the spring of 1959 on two bills—S. 838 proposed by Senator Joseph C. O'Mahoney of Wyoming and S. 839 proposed by Senators Estes Kefauver of Tennessee and the late Thomas C. Hennings Jr. of Missouri. Again the evidence was overwhelming that some action should be taken. Neither proposal, however, has become law at this writing.

Strengthen or Enact State Laws That Protect the Consumer. A number of states have passed legislation that protects the consumer in the all-too-complicated world of buying on time. For example, the New York State Law, the first to protect the consumer in practically all types of time sales, does the following: places a limit on credit service charges, requires all charges be clearly itemized, requires the seller to give the buyer a copy of the contract, forbids the taking of a contract signed in blank, gives the consumer the right to prepay his account at any time and get credit for unearned charges, prohibits "fine print" and defines and limits revolving credit plans. However, despite the progress being made in consumers' rights legislation, a large number of states either have no laws or the laws they do have are totally inadequate. For example, about half the states have no laws that set a maximum finance rate the consumer can be charged when he buys a new car. This means that consumers in nearly half the states can be charged any finance rate the unscrupulous dealer or sales finance company thinks it can get away with. Further, there are at least seven states that have set such high limits that they virtually legalize the activities of the dealer who picks the public's pocket. I might add no state has passed legislation that would make the seller of credit tell the consumer the cost of credit in terms of simple annual interest.

Support a State Consumer Counsel. The enactment of consumer protective legislation will prove meaningless unless we are told how the laws work and are educated in the intricacies of debt buying. One way this can be done is through the creation of State Consumer Counsels. Such offices, or variations, already exist in California, Connecticut, Massachusetts, New York and New Jersey. The governors of Minnesota and Michigan proposed consumer counsels for their states, but the state legislatures failed to adopt the necessary laws. The typical State Consumer Counsel is not only concerned with time buying, but all areas of consumer complaints and protection. In calling for a consumer counsel in his inaugural message to the California Legislature, Governor Edmund G. Brown declared: "We are all consumers. Yet, we have never been able to speak in a single voice because we are disorganized and our needs are so diverse. Without a forceful spokesman in government, we have little defense against highly organized special interests. I therefore recommend the appointment of a Consumers' Advocate." Helen Ewing Nelson, California's Consumer Counsel, reported that out of the myriad complaints her office has received, the largest number concerned the cost of debt.

Interestingly, the Consumer Counsel idea was pioneered by former Governor Averill Harriman of New York and Dr. Persia Campbell, who has probably done more for the consumer than any other person in the United States. Governor Harriman originated the nation's first Consumer Counsel in 1955 and Dr. Campbell held the office. It was abolished, however, when Nelson Rockefeller succeeded Harriman as governor. As a result, New York's consumer protection activities were established in the State Banking Department and the Bureau of Consumer Frauds and Protection in the State Department of Law, under the direction of Attorney General Louis J. Lefkowitz. Despite the overlapping and confusion to the time buyer who may not know where to go, the attorney general is doing some excellent work in protecting the consumer.*

Wherever Possible Join or Start a Credit Union. Of all the people I have talked to while gathering material for this book, no group has impressed me as much as those associated with the credit union movement. I have visited credit unions with less than five thousand dollars and others with as much as one million dollars in assets. I have talked to men who have devoted almost their entire lives to credit unions and others who are just discovering the hope they represent. I have gone to their leaders' homes, walked the streets with them, visited with their members. These are selfless individuals with one purpose—helping people help each other.

---

* According to the attorney general's office, the Bureau of Consumer Frauds and Protection, established by Lefkowitz, was the first State agency of its kind with enforcement powers. The Bureau also conducts an intensive campaign to educate the consumer.

A credit union is simply a group of people who save their money together and make loans to each other at low interest rates. (The maximum is 12 per cent true annual interest.) Currently there are nearly twenty thousand such cooperative societies in the United States, with over eleven million members, roughly 6 per cent of the population. Their assets total over four billion, eight hundred million dollars and their loans outstanding come to more than three billion, six hundred million dollars. Those who have saved and borrowed this money include government employees, teachers, laborers, production and white collar workers, veterans' groups and church organizations. Each credit union is organized by members of a particular group, such as people who work for the same employer or who belong to the same fraternal order, church, labor union, or who live in the same community. Although credit union policies are set by the individual membership or by their elected representatives, each group functions under a state or federal charter and their financial operations are reviewed and supervised by the government.

Credit unions do two things. They teach people the value of thrift, paying dividends on the money saved, and they lend money to their members for any good purpose, including payment of old bills, funerals, vacations, automobiles, education and family emergencies. Some make mortgage loans out of surplus funds. Most loans are made on the borrowers' signatures and it is not uncommon for credit unions to take so-called risks where commercial institutions would be afraid to venture. Despite this liberal policy, 99½ per cent of all loans are repaid. The credit union people contend that loyalty to the other members accounts for this remarkable figure. Finally, it should be pointed out that although credit unions are non-profit organizations, they do not conflict with commercial lenders but complement and supplement the operations of private business. For the credit unions themselves their main business is to meet their members' needs for consumer credit.*

Shop Around for Credit. It is amazing how many people who buy on time willingly accept whatever terms are offered them. Comparison shopping is an old American tradition. It is even more important when you buy on credit than when you pay cash. If you don't understand the terms, you might find yourself tied to a contract that will pull you down into financial bankruptcy. And don't let anyone overload you with debt. No matter what you may be told, there is nothing easy about "easy credit." Remember, whenever you can afford it, pay cash.

The final appeal must be made to the debt merchants themselves. It is within their power to end the terrible excesses that have been brought about by the consumer credit explosion. Many of them, I know, have attempted to minimize these excesses. Others, however, have found the merchandising of debt a lucrative treasure-trove for legalized plunder. The human tragedy and indignities that have resulted have no place in a free society.

Let it not be said that America, in the midst of plenty, suffered its citizens to become a nation of indentured debtors.

---

* If you wish to join or start a credit union, you may obtain the necessary information by writing Credit Union National Association, Madison 1, Wisconsin.

Appendix

The following formula, called the constant ratio method, is one of the easiest ways of calculating the annual interest rate. It can be used to determine simple annual interest on installment contracts where the time payments are made over a twelve-month period or over odd periods like nine months, eighteen months, thirty-two months.

This is the formula:

$$r = \frac{2pC}{A(n+1)}$$

r = the annual interest rate

p = number of payment periods *in one year* exclusive of the down payment. (Always 12 if monthly payments made, 4 if quarterly payments, 52 if weekly payments.)

C = the interest or finance charge in dollars

A = the amount borrowed

n = the number of equal installment payments in the whole contract period exclusive of the down payment.

This is how the formula is used. Ralph Homer buys an automobile for $2,600. His down payment is $800. The dealer computes the finance charge at $135. Ralph Homer agrees to pay the sum owed in fifteen equal monthly installments. What is the simple annual interest rate?

Let us insert the figures into the formula:
  $p = 12$ (number of payment periods in one year)
  $C = \$135$ (the interest or finance charge in dollars)
  $A = \$1,800$ ($2,600 minus the $800 down payment)
  $n = 15$ (the number of equal installment payments in the whole contract.)

Here is the formula with the figures inserted:

$$r = \frac{2 \text{ times } 12 \text{ times } \$135}{\$1,800 \text{ times } (15 \text{ plus } 1)} = \frac{\$3,240}{\$28,800} = 11.3 \text{ per cent}$$

Thus the answer in terms of simple annual interest is 11.3 per cent. It should be noted that the constant ratio method tends to overstate the actual rate somewhat. Though the results therefore are approximate, the formula itself is comparatively simple.

The credit seller instead of quoting you finance charges in dollars and cents may give you the carrying charge by quoting an interest figure. The following true annual interest tables were presented to the people of California, by that state's Consumer Counsel. Here's what you pay for credit:

If it is added to the purchase price and the total is repaid in 12 equal monthly payments:

When they say	you pay in true annual interest
4% per year	7.3%
6% per year	10.9%
8% per year	14.5%

10% per year	18.0%
1% per month	21.5%

If it is charged only on the unpaid balance:

When they say	you pay in true annual interest
¾ of 1% per month:	9%
⅚ of 1% per month:	10%
1% per month:	12%
1¼% per month:	15%
1½% per month:	18%
2½% per month:	30%

If you wish to learn the *dollar* cost of credit, you do the following:

Step One: Multiply the monthly or weekly payment by the number of months or weeks the payments are to be made. The result is the total amount of your installment payments.

Step Two: Add the down payment to the total of your installment payments.

Step Three: Subtract the cash price from the total of your installment payments plus your down payment. The difference is the cost of credit in *dollars*.

Let us return to Ralph Homer, who decided to buy a desk on time. The down payment was $12. He also agreed to pay $10 a month for twelve months. If he had paid cash, the desk would have cost him $120. What was Ralph's dollar cost of credit?

Step One: Multiply $10 (his monthly installment payment) times 12 (the number of months he made the payments). This comes to $120.

Step Two: Add $12 (the down payment) to $120 (the total of Ralph's monthly installment payments). The answer is $132.

Step Three: Subtract $120 (the cash price) from $132 (Ralph's total monthly installments plus the down payment). The difference is $12, the sum Ralph paid in *dollars* for credit. To put it another way, Ralph would have saved $12 if he had paid cash.

Index